THE FUNDAMENTAL ROLE OF
SCIENCE AND
TECHNOLOGY IN
INTERNATIONAL
DEVELOPMENT

AN IMPERATIVE FOR THE U.S. AGENCY
FOR INTERNATIONAL DEVELOPMENT

Committee on Science and Technology in Foreign Assistance
Office for Central Europe and Eurasia
Development, Security, and Cooperation
Policy and Global Affairs

NATIONAL RESEARCH COUNCIL
OF THE NATIONAL ACADEMIES

D1449664

THE NATIONAL ACADEMIES PRESS
Washington, D.C.
www.nap.edu

THE NATIONAL ACADEMIES PRESS • 500 Fifth Street, N.W. • Washington, D.C. 20001

NOTICE: The project that is the subject of this report was approved by the Governing Board of the National Research Council, whose members are drawn from the councils of the National Academy of Sciences, the National Academy of Engineering, and the Institute of Medicine. The members of the committee responsible for the report were chosen for their special competences and with regard for appropriate balance.

This study was supported by the U.S. Agency for International Development, the Bill & Melinda Gates Foundation, the Sloan Foundation, and the Presidents' Committee. Any opinions, findings, conclusions, or recommendations expressed in this publication are those of the authors and do not necessarily reflect the views of the organizations or agencies that provided support for the project.

One copy of this report per request is available from the Office for Central Europe and Eurasia, National Research Council, 500 Fifth Street, N.W., Washington, DC 20001; (202) 334-2644; Fax (202) 334-2614

Additional copies of this report are available from the National Academies Press, 500 Fifth Street, N.W., Lockbox 285, Washington, DC 20055; (800) 624-6242 or (202) 334-3313 (in the Washington metropolitan area); Internet, http://www.nap.edu.

International Standard Book Number 0-309-10145-X (Book)
International Standard Book Number 0-309-65859-4 (PDF)
Library of Congress Control Number 2001012345

Cover photos courtesy of U.S. Agency for International Develoment

THE NATIONAL ACADEMIES
Advisers to the Nation on Science, Engineering, and Medicine

The **National Academy of Sciences** is a private, nonprofit, self-perpetuating society of distinguished scholars engaged in scientific and engineering research, dedicated to the furtherance of science and technology and to their use for the general welfare. Upon the authority of the charter granted to it by the Congress in 1863, the Academy has a mandate that requires it to advise the federal government on scientific and technical matters. Dr. Ralph J. Cicerone is president of the National Academy of Sciences.

The **National Academy of Engineering** was established in 1964, under the charter of the National Academy of Sciences, as a parallel organization of outstanding engineers. It is autonomous in its administration and in the selection of its members, sharing with the National Academy of Sciences the responsibility for advising the federal government. The National Academy of Engineering also sponsors engineering programs aimed at meeting national needs, encourages education and research, and recognizes the superior achievements of engineers. Dr. Wm. A. Wulf is president of the National Academy of Engineering.

The **Institute of Medicine** was established in 1970 by the National Academy of Sciences to secure the services of eminent members of appropriate professions in the examination of policy matters pertaining to the health of the public. The Institute acts under the responsibility given to the National Academy of Sciences by its congressional charter to be an adviser to the federal government and, upon its own initiative, to identify issues of medical care, research, and education. Dr. Harvey V. Fineberg is president of the Institute of Medicine.

The **National Research Council** was organized by the National Academy of Sciences in 1916 to associate the broad community of science and technology with the Academy's purposes of furthering knowledge and advising the federal government. Functioning in accordance with general policies determined by the Academy, the Council has become the principal operating agency of both the National Academy of Sciences and the National Academy of Engineering in providing services to the government, the public, and the scientific and engineering communities. The Council is administered jointly by both Academies and the Institute of Medicine. Dr. Ralph J. Cicerone and Dr. Wm. A. Wulf are chair and vice chair, respectively, of the National Research Council.

www.national-academies.org

Preface

In October 2003 the U.S. Agency for International Development (USAID) and the National Research Council (NRC) entered into a cooperative agreement that called for the NRC to examine selected aspects of U.S. foreign assistance activities—primarily the programs of USAID—that have benefited or could benefit from access to strong science, technology, and medical capabilities in the United States or elsewhere. After consideration of many aspects of the role of science and technology (S&T) in foreign assistance, the study led to recommendations for specific programmatic, organizational, and personnel reforms that would increase the effective use of S&T to meet USAID's goals while supporting larger U.S. foreign policy objectives. The statement of task is set forth in Appendix A.

Shortly after the cooperative agreement was developed, additional financial support for the study was obtained from three other organizations. The NRC provided funds available from private sources. The Bill & Melinda Gates Foundation also provided substantial support. Then, at the request of the Science and Technology Adviser to the Secretary of State, the Sloan Foundation contributed supplemental funding.

According to USAID officials, the agency's interest in initiating a fresh examination of a topic that has been on the foreign assistance agenda for decades was rooted in several recent developments. These developments included the advent of new technologies that were sensitizing governments and populations to the benefits of appropriate use of these technologies (e.g., deployment of global positioning satellite systems, advances in genetic engineering, and developments in nanotechnology). At the same time, the agency recognized that many well-established technologies would remain of great importance throughout the developing world for decades to come. In addition, problems in the developing countries that could be moderated through effective use of S&T increasingly affect the United States (infectious diseases, global environmental problems, and protection of intellectual property rights, for example). Finally, using technologies effectively in anticipating and responding to natural disasters, such as earthquakes, tsunamis, hurricanes, droughts, and floods, remains a high priority for the agency.

According to senior USAID officials, two other developments also played a role in raising the interest of the USAID leadership in investments in S&T. The World Bank, other donor governments, and private foundations, particularly the Gates Foundation, were increasing their interests in S&T. All the while, a large number of U.S. government departments and agencies were expanding S&T-oriented activities in developing countries that increasingly overlapped with USAID program interests.

The following reports concerning the importance of S&T in international affairs in general and in international development in particular were also cited by USAID officials as being of considerable interest.

• In 1999 the NRC issued a privately funded report entitled *The Pervasive Role of Science, Technology, and Health in Foreign Policy: Imperatives for the Department of State.*
• In 2001 the RAND Corporation issued a report prepared for the World Bank entitled *Science and Technology Collaborations: Building Capacity in Developing Countries.*
• In 2002 USAID asked the RAND Corporation to extend the work it had done for the World Bank by carrying out consultations with three USAID missions, which led to the report *USAID and Science and Technology Capacity Building for Development.*

Against this background of new interest in the topic, senior officials of the NRC and USAID became engaged in a series of meetings and informal discussions to review recent reports and to consider the opportunities for integrating S&T considerations more fully into the international development process. These discussions led to the present report.

The NRC has had extensive experience in addressing S&T issues within the framework of international development. Over the last four decades the National Academies has issued numerous reports on this topic and carried out a number of projects with developing country counterparts. A list of the recent reports that are particularly relevant to this study is included in Appendix I. Other relevant NRC activities that are underway are identified in Appendix J.

The NRC appointed a multidisciplinary committee of experts in international affairs and foreign assistance, and particularly S&T activities, to carry out this study. The committee members are identified in Appendix B.

Initially, the committee surveyed a broad range of USAID activities. These activities included programs supported by funds appropriated for development assistance, child survival and health, humanitarian assistance, economic security support, and stabilization and reconstruction efforts in war-torn countries. As the study progressed and after consulting with USAID, the committee decided to focus its efforts largely on development assistance and child survival and health while still taking into account other USAID activities. The committee believes that building appropriate S&T capacity is central to long-term development of countries where USAID has programs. However, the budget for development assistance has been on the decline despite the rapid growth of other types of assistance. The committee considered that an emphasis on development assistance would help the U.S. Executive Branch and the Congress assess whether the budget decline has been in the national interest.

The committee, in consultation with USAID officials, selected for analysis five important problems that exemplify the range of S&T-related issues confronting large numbers of developing countries:

1. Child survival;
2. Safe water;
3. Agricultural research;
4. Microeconomic reform; and
5. Natural disasters.

The purpose of analyzing these problems, which cut across a range of social and environmental concerns, was to help identify categories of administrative and technical issues that should be addressed in assessing USAID's overall capabilities to use S&T effectively.

Small teams of committee members, NRC staff, and other experts visited six countries where USAID supports significant activities that have considerable S&T content. The purpose of the visits was to obtain field insights on the role of S&T in foreign assistance, with a focus on the practical aspects of carrying out S&T-related projects in different overseas environments. The countries and the topics of focus were:

- India: health care;
- Bangladesh: agriculture and food security;
- Philippines: energy and environment;
- Guatemala and El Salvador: biodiversity; and
- Mali: poverty in a resource-deficient country.

In each country, consultations were held with senior officials and specialists from USAID and other U.S. government departments and agencies, with local officials and specialists, and with project managers working for USAID partners. The visiting teams concentrated on the likely impacts of current USAID programs and particularly the importance of S&T contributions to the effectiveness of the programs. It was important, of course, to consider these programs within the context of the host country's priorities, related activities of other donors, and activities of other U.S. government departments and agencies. The reports prepared following the visits can be obtained from the public access file of the NRC by contacting pkoshel@nas.edu.

Another important source of information was the report of USAID's Worldwide Mission Directors Conference held in May 2005. Conclusions from the conference are included in this report.

Throughout the study the committee members and staff consulted with representatives of many USAID offices in Washington (see Appendix D). The views of USAID partners and independent experts in the United States as well as in the field have been of considerable importance to the committee, and these contacts are identified in Appendix E.

During the process the committee was mindful of the importance of successful projects that demonstrate approaches that work. Appendix H presents a few projects that have been identified by USAID as having been of particular interest.

In September 2004 the committee issued an interim report outlining its general approach to the study. In response, several USAID offices, 10 USAID missions, and other organizations offered their observations concerning the direction the study was taking. These responses were considered in preparing the present report, and some of the observations that were provided are included in the body of this report.

After reviewing the many inputs received, the committee decided to devote Chapter 1 of this report to describing the context for the role of S&T in foreign assistance, drawing on the interim report and on other observations during the course of the study. Chapter 2 discusses the five problem areas selected for special attention. The conclusions and recommendations of the report are then set forth in three chapters. Chapter 3 presents suggestions as to USAID's role in strengthening the capacity of developing countries to select and adapt existing and emerging technologies to their needs and to develop the human resource, policy, and facility infrastructures that are essential to use S&T effectively in the development process. Chapter 4 is devoted to USAID's internal capability to use S&T expertise effectively in developing and managing its programs in ways that respond to developing country needs and priorities. Chapter 5 considers the integration of USAID programs and interests with the activities of other U.S. government departments and agencies. In this regard, an estimated 40 departments and agencies have active programs in developing countries, with financial resources provided by USAID or through their own congressional appropriations.

ACKNOWLEDGMENTS

Many important aspects of foreign assistance could not be addressed adequately within the constraints of time and funds available for this study: for example, the significance of S&T in reconstruction efforts supported by USAID and other donors in Iraq, Afghanistan, and other war-torn areas was not addressed. The roles of international organizations, development banks, and other bilateral donors in supporting S&T-related activities and coordination of their activities with USAID's efforts certainly deserve more attention. The contributions to development of technology-oriented multinational companies and of the private sectors of the developing countries themselves should be elaborated. Philanthropic and nongovernmental organizations are only briefly mentioned. The field visits were extraordinarily important, and additional visits would provide many new insights into the USAID experience in drawing on the S&T strengths of the United States in developing program strategies and in designing, implementing, and evaluating projects.

Many USAID staff members and partners at headquarters and in the field assisted the committee. We especially appreciated the insights offered by Andrew Natsios, the former Administrator, who clearly recognizes the need to strengthen the use of science and technology in the agency's development activities. We would also like to thank Gary Bittner, Emmy Simmons, Anne Peterson, John Grayzel, John Becker, and Neal Brandes for their support. Rosalyn Hobson, now at Virginia Commonwealth University and a former American Association for the Advancement of Science Fellow at USAID, deserves special thanks for guiding the committee members and staff through the many relevant offices within USAID and providing excellent advice about the development context for USAID activities during the field visits. In addition, special appreciation is due Craig Meisner, who was responsible for organizing the site visit in Bangladesh.

Several experts who accompanied members of the committee on the field visits and who provided general guidance to the committee greatly enriched the quality of the report: Michael Clegg, Foreign Secretary of the National Academy of Sciences and Professor, University of California, Irvine; Charles Hess, University of California, Davis; Anthony Stocks, Idaho State University; Helen Smits, Institute of Medicine; John Lewis, ProNatura USA; and Geoffrey Dabelko, Woodrow Wilson International Center.

This report has been reviewed in draft form by individuals chosen for their diverse perspectives and technical expertise, in accordance with procedures approved by the NRC's Report Review Committee. The purpose of this independent review is to provide candid and critical comments that will assist the institution in making its published report as sound as possible and to ensure that the report meets institutional standards for objectivity, evidence, and responsiveness to the study charge. The review comments and draft manuscript remain confidential to protect the integrity of the process.

We wish to thank the following individuals for their review of this report: Robert Black, Johns Hopkins University; Patrick Cronin, Center for Strategic and International Studies; John Daly, Consultant; Kerri-Ann Jones, National Science Foundation; Princeton Lyman, Council on Foreign Relations; Robert Tropp,

Washington Development Capital Corporation; Charles Weiss, Georgetown University; Charles Wilson, Independent Consultant; and Tilahun Yilma, University of California, Davis.

Although the reviewers listed above provided many constructive comments and suggestions, they were not asked to endorse the conclusions or recommendations, nor did they see the final draft of the report before its release. The review of this report was overseen by Enriqueta Bond, Burroughs Wellcome Fund, and Norman Neureiter, American Association for the Advancement of Science. Appointed by the NRC, they were responsible for making certain that an independent examination of this report was carried out in accordance with institutional procedures and that all review comments were carefully considered. Responsibility for the final content of this report rests entirely with the authoring committee and the institution.

Glenn Schweitzer and Pat Koshel provided able support for the entire study effort and for the report preparation. The committee was also assisted by a number of other staff members of the NRC including Laura Holliday and Sara Gray. Zainep Mahmoud, an Anderson Intern, and Suzanne Goh and Eric Bone, Christine Mirzayan Fellows, also aided the committee.

Thomas R. Pickering
Kenneth Shine
Co-chairs
Committee on Science and Technology
in Foreign Assistance

Contents

Summary

Science and technology (S&T) capabilities are fundamental for social and economic progress in developing countries; for example, in the health sector, scientific research led to the development and introduction of oral rehydration therapy, which became the cornerstone of international efforts to control diarrheal diseases. Research also established that two cents worth of vitamin A given to children every six months could reduce child mortality in many countries by over one-third. In agriculture, rice-wheat rotation techniques have significantly enhanced food production in South Asia. In Central America, scientifically based natural resource management has been essential in developing the tourist industry, a major source of foreign currency.

International programs based on S&T are critical components of U.S. foreign policy, and particularly foreign assistance activities. Foreign assistance, probably more than any other international endeavor, provides opportunities for representatives of the U.S. government and its partners to join with political and economic leaders, intellectuals, and activists of dozens of countries in continuing, constructive dialogues and in concrete projects designed to enhance the quality of life of hundreds of millions of people. S&T are often the keystones for successful projects. The shared political and economic dividends from these activities can be enormous.

Maintaining and strengthening the contributions of the science, engineering, and medical capabilities of the United States to foreign assistance programs administered by the U.S. Agency for International Development (USAID) are the themes of this report. USAID has unique and broad legislative authority to support innovative programs in developing countries, unrivaled field experience in adapting technological advances to conditions and capabilities of poor countries, and many successes in integrating S&T into development activities. Therefore, as S&T capabilities become even more important for all countries in addressing traditional development issues and in coping with increased international flows of goods and services and the rapid spread of diseases and contaminants, the agency should play a central role in promoting the S&T-related programs of the U.S. government throughout the developing world.

Unfortunately, many developing countries, particularly the poor countries of Africa, do not have the human resources, physical and economic infrastructures, and access to capital to take full advantage of the S&T expertise and achievements of the United States and other industrialized countries. Nevertheless, countries at all levels of development have a strong desire for more robust S&T capabilities. And some capability to understand the potential and limitations of S&T, to select and effectively utilize suitable foreign technologies, and to develop local innovations is needed in every country.

The observations and recommendations set forth below on the opportunities for USAID to continue to play an important role in bringing to bear the S&T resources of the United States on foreign assistance programs are based on extensive consultations by the committee of the National Research Council (NRC) responsible for this report. The members and staff met with many government officials, foreign assistance practitioners, and S&T specialists in the United States and abroad. The committee sent small teams to six developing countries where USAID has significant programs. These countries and areas of special interest during the field visits were:

1. India: health;
2. Philippines: energy;
3. Bangladesh: agriculture and food security;
4. Guatemala and El Salvador: biodiversity; and
5. Mali: poverty in a resource-deficient country.

To help ensure that the conclusions of this report have broad significance, the committee addressed five development challenges that affect hundreds of millions of people each year. These challenges are:

1. Child survival;
2 Safe water;
3. Agricultural research;
4. Microeconomic reform; and
5. Prevention of and response to natural disasters.

International approaches to providing assistance to developing countries are changing; for example, global programs with important S&T dimensions that target health, food production, environmental, and other problems omnipresent in the developing countries are growing in number and size while bilateral assistance is also increasing. A particularly important challenge for USAID is to find its role amidst the expanding network of dozens of foreign assistance providers, and particularly those providers of S&T-related assistance that draws on the limited capabilities of recipient countries to manage technology-oriented programs.

Beyond foreign assistance funds provided by governments, other financial flows to developing countries with S&T implications are growing. They include foreign direct investment by the private sector, remittances to friends and relatives in developing countries sent home by émigrés who are resident in the industrialized countries, contributions to development projects by private foundations, and initiatives designed to benefit local populations supported by multinational companies. At the same time, some donors and international banks are canceling debt repayment obligations of a few poor countries, thereby enhancing the ability of these countries to invest more in education, agriculture, and other activities essential to long-term development.

Private flows often support technical education and vocational training. Private foundations sometimes support long-term research programs in search of breakthroughs, and Table S-1 presents an important example in this regard. Of special significance are public-private partnerships in mobilizing financial and technological resources for use in poor countries. For example, results achieved by the Global Development Alliance, which links USAID and many private company capabilities, have demonstrated the positive affects of well-designed technology-oriented partnerships.

Meanwhile, within the U.S. government the responsibilities for programs in developing countries are rapidly diffusing, with USAID now financing only about 50 percent of the government's international development programs. The independent Millennium Challenge Corporation (MCC), which was established by the U.S. government in 2002, has a multibillion-dollar development program directed to 23 countries although it has been slow in launching its initial projects. The Department of State has relatively new responsibilities for programs directed to combating HIV/AIDS, also with an annual budget in the billions of dollars. Its HIV/AIDS program is moving forward very quickly while a number of other U.S. departments and agencies, international organizations, and private foundations finance directly related activities (see Figure S-1).

A new office in the Department of State is responsible for planning and coordinating reconstruction activities following hostilities in countries around the globe. In addition to USAID, the Department of Defense continues to be a major contributor to reconstruction efforts in war-torn countries and plays an important role in responding to humanitarian disasters. Many other departments and agencies, including the Centers for Disease Control and Prevention, the Department of Agriculture, the Environmental Protection Agency, and the Department of Energy, have expanded the international dimensions of their mission-

TABLE S-1 The Bill & Melinda Gates Foundation's Grand Challenges to Global Health

Long-Term Goal to Improve Health in the Developing World	Associated Grand Challenges
Improve childhood vaccines	• Create effective single-dose vaccines • Prepare vaccines that do not require refrigeration • Develop needle-free vaccine delivery systems
Create new vaccines	• Devise testing systems for new vaccines • Design antigens for protective immunity • Learn about immunological response
Control insects that transmit agents of disease	• Develop genetic strategy to control insects • Develop chemical strategy to control insects
Improve nutrition to promote health	• Create a nutrient-rich staple plant series
Improve drug treatment of infectious diseases	• Find drugs and delivery systems to limit drug resistance
Cure latent and chronic infection	• Create therapies that can cure latent infection • Create immunological methods to cure latent infection
Measure health status accurately and economically in developing countries	• Develop technologies to assess population health • Develop versatile diagnostic tools

SOURCE: Gates Foundation, August 2005.

oriented activities that potentially overlap with traditional development activities; and a large fraction of these programs have substantial S&T components.

Within this myriad of expanding activities, USAID supports hundreds of foreign assistance projects. But its role in carrying out its program is increasingly determined by dozens of congressional earmarks and White House initiatives, including many with S&T components. Some earmarks sustain important programs, but too often, earmarks do not have high development dividends when they focus on narrow special interests.

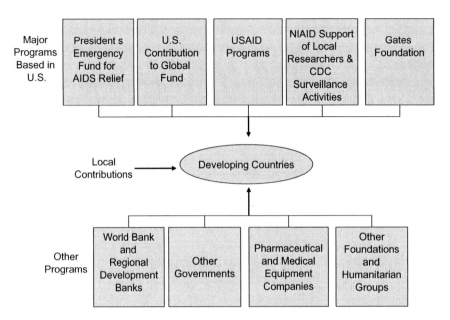

FIGURE S-1 Organizations involved in combating HIV/AIDS in developing countries.

In recent years, the agency has lost much of its direct-hire staff with technical expertise while other government departments and agencies with much stronger expertise in specific areas of interest to these organizations are expanding their activities in developing countries. This decline of technical expertise is the single most important reason why USAID has lost much of its S&T capability and reputation, which is critical in providing leadership in applying S&T to overcome development problems. Strong USAID internal capabilities are essential to guide the effective use of S&T resources in agency programs and to work collaboratively on problems of common interest with other organizations that have well-established technical capabilities.

Since S&T are integral components of many foreign assistance activities, consideration of USAID's efforts to draw on the nation's S&T capabilities must begin with consideration of USAID's broader role in foreign assistance. USAID will, of course, continue to follow the decisions of the Administration and Congress to support program activities in many fields within USAID's established program framework of governance and humanitarian assistance, reconstruction in war-torn areas, global health, and broadly defined economic growth; however, the agency should to the extent possible select a few areas of emphasis within this framework where it can concentrate resources and be an international leader in addition to its well-established leadership role in promoting democratic governance. Criteria for selecting such areas should include (1) high levels of developing country interest, (2) opportunities to have significant impacts on development, (3) relevance of USAID's unique field experience, and (4) limited interest of other U.S. departments and agencies in providing substantial financial support for activities in the areas.

Programs in some or all of these areas will undoubtedly require substantial S&T inputs. One area for possible emphasis is health delivery systems, an area that the committee strongly supports. Other examples that the committee believes should be considered are small innovative firms, agriculture extension, and information technology. The program emphasis within each area should be on institution building, including establishment of research, education, training, and service capabilities.

In order to continue to support its current portfolio of programs as well as new activities, USAID needs stronger in-house technical staff capabilities. Given rigid congressional limitations on personnel levels, the agency will have no choice in the near term but to continue to rely heavily on a combination of direct-hire employees, assignees from other U.S. agencies, and contractor personnel to manage programs implemented by USAID's partners. Nevertheless, as recommended in this report, the agency should recruit an adequate number of technically trained direct-hire employees to lead the design and evaluation of institution building and innovation activities, particularly in the areas of emphasis that are selected.

Against this background, the committee offers three overarching recommendations for consideration by USAID, the Department of State, the Office of Management and Budget, Congress, and other interested organizations. Suggestions of specific steps for implementing the recommendations are also set forth. The recommendations, if implemented, would strengthen USAID's capabilities to play a more effective role in supporting technical innovation as a key to successful international development.

Most of the suggestions are general and cut across development sectors. As noted above, while carrying out the agency's many programs mandated by Congress and the White House, USAID should also begin to focus on several areas of emphasis and concentrate available resources in these areas within the framework of the recommendations that are set forth below.

Recommendation 1: *USAID should reverse the decline in its support for building S&T capacity within important development sectors in developing countries.* Clearly, development of human resources and building relevant institutions must be at the top of the priority list if nations are to have the ability to develop, adapt, and introduce technological innovations in sectors of importance to their governments, the private sector, and their populations. To this end, USAID should:

  • Increase the number of USAID-sponsored participants in highly focused graduate training programs to develop future leaders in various S&T disciplines;

• Increase financial support for applied research and outreach, including extension, at local institutions that can support host country priority programs of interest to USAID;

• Provide increased financial support for development of local capacity to deliver public health services, including support for the establishment of strong schools of public health in developing countries;

• Assist important institutions in developing countries in using broadband access to Internet and other modern technologies to strengthen their information acquisition and processing capabilities in support of S&T specialists; and

• Sponsor expert assessments of the S&T infrastructures in countries where USAID has major programs when there are interested customers for such assessments.

Recommendation 2: *USAID should strengthen the capabilities of its leadership and program managers in Washington and in the field to recognize and take advantage of opportunities for effectively integrating S&T considerations within USAID programs.* The following steps by USAID would help achieve this objective.

• Development of an S&T culture within USAID, with the agency leadership continually articulating in policy papers, internal discussions, and interactions with host governments the importance of (1) strengthening local S&T capabilities, (2) integrating these capabilities within a broad range of development activities, and (3) incorporating S&T in USAID programs;

• Strengthening of USAID staff capabilities in S&T through (1) recruitment of senior officials with strong S&T credentials and good project management track records, (2) an increased number of entry-level positions devoted to young professionals with S&T expertise, and (3) **career incentives** for technically trained employees to remain at USAID, and particularly, promotion opportunities based on an individual's success in applying technical skills to USAID programs; and

• Appointment of a full-time S&T adviser to the administrator, with adequate staff, to alert the USAID leadership and program managers on a continuing basis to overlooked and new opportunities for programs with significant S&T content. Figure S-2 suggests how the adviser might be positioned within the agency.

• Establishment of an independent S&T advisory mechanism to address technical issues of interest to the USAID leadership and to promote peer review throughout the agency (see Figure S-2);

• Establishment of a nongovernmental Innovation Center to concentrate on application of innovative technologies to specific development problems identified by USAID missions, USAID Washington, and the Center's staff (see Figure S-2);

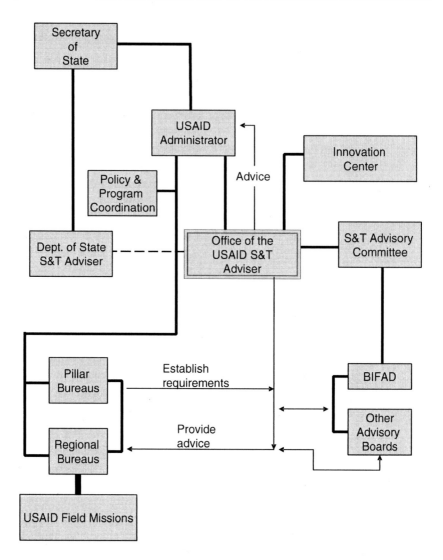

FIGURE S-2 Strengthening the organizational structure for S&T in USAID.

• Strengthening the economic analysis capability of USAID to help ensure that the many dimensions of technological change occurring in almost every developing country are adequately considered when designing and implementing agency projects; and

• Revitalizing the program evaluation capability of USAID using rigorous methodologies to gauge program effectiveness.

Recommendation 3. *USAID should encourage other U.S. government de-partments and agencies with S&T-related activities in developing countries to orient their programs to the extent possible to supporting the development priorities of the host countries, and USAID should provide leadership in im-proving interagency coordination of activities relevant to development.* USAID's long history of working in developing countries provides the agency with unique field perspectives, but it is not as strong as other departments and agencies in many technological areas. Its capabilities should be effectively inte-grated with the well-developed S&T capabilities of other U.S. government orga-nizations. To that end, USAID should:

• Assume leadership, in cooperation with the Department of State and the Office of Science and Technology Policy, in the establishment in Washington of an effective interagency committee to coordinate the overlapping S&T interests of U.S. departments and agencies in developing countries;
• Emphasize within the joint State-USAID planning process and in the field the payoff from broad interagency coordination of S&T-related activities;
• Clarify the division of responsibilities for supporting research relevant to international development supported by USAID and other U.S. government de-partments and agencies. Table S-2 presents a suggested role for USAID in the health sector;
• Work with other government organizations that are involved in prevent-ing and responding to natural disasters with an expanded emphasis on the capac-ity of developing countries to improve early warning systems, upgrade the resil-ience of physical structures to impacts, increase availability of emergency social support resources, and develop hazard mitigation and emergency response strat-egies that can be integrated with long-term development programs;
• Work closely with the Departments of State and Defense and other na-tional and international organizations involved in reconstruction of war-torn ar-eas, taking advantage of the technical capabilities of these partners while sharing USAID's field experience in charting the course for recovery;
• Develop USAID programs that complement the programs of the Depart-ment of State for combating HIV/AIDS, tuberculosis, and malaria, capitalizing on USAID's unique field experience to build local capacity for delivering health services; and
• Encourage the Millennium Challenge Corporation (MCC) to take advan-tage of USAID's many years of experience in promoting international develop-ment in the countries where the MCC has initiated programs.

USAID has recorded many achievements in using S&T to overcome ob-stacles to development; for example, support of effective policies for integrating energy networks has brought electrical power to thousands of remote villages in South Africa. In Namibia a USAID partnership with Microsoft and Compaq has

TABLE S-4 Improving Health Outcomes: Role of USAID in the New Global Landscape for Research on Special Problems of Developing Countries

	Health Assessment/ Priority Setting	Basic Research	Applied Research/Development/ Adaptation	Field Implementation and Evaluation
Task	Disease surveillance Assessments of burden of disease Identification of Critical Knowledge Gaps		Product development Field trials Consumer research Modification of existing products	Adaptation at scale Strengthening national health systems Monitor program effectiveness and modify approaches
Performance	Local agencies **USAID** (major)/ CDC Bilateral donors	NIH Pharmaceutical companies International foundations Local research organizations	Pharmaceutical and medical supply companies Local research organizations **USAID** Bilateral donors	Local agencies **USAID** (major) Global fund WHO Bilateral donors PEPFAR

Improved Health Outcomes

developed effective e-government services and has dramatically enhanced civil participation in parliamentary affairs.

Now, the challenge is for the entire agency to recognize more fully the opportunities to integrate one of America's strongest assets—S&T—into foreign assistance and to transform this recognition into action programs in the field. The U.S. government faces many new issues in developing countries, from countering terrorism, implementing policies of the World Trade Organization, and addressing global environmental threats, to improving America's image. U.S. S&T capabilities can help equip USAID to address such issues while also building bridges of mutual understanding that will far transcend traditional concepts of the payoffs to the United States from investments in foreign assistance.

Realization of this vision will not be easy. In the competition for access to limited foreign assistance funds, important constituencies of USAID that embrace basic human needs as the overriding priority have never accepted the approach of technology transfer, stimulation of economic growth, and diffusion of benefits to the general population from innovative nodes in the economy and in society. Nevertheless, with the upsurge in the foreign assistance budget and the globalization of problems, institutions, and solutions, there should be an opportunity for the private voluntary organizations to have funding for their grassroots programs and for USAID to simultaneously undertake serious S&T investments for long-term economic growth.

The entire foreign assistance establishment must be persuaded that S&T are crucial enablers of development and not simply endpoints. Just as governance has become a significant rationale for much of America's global presence, so S&T must be recognized as an essential platform for transforming aspirations for better lives into durable and practical reality. Only then will the sustainability of a strong S&T component within USAID be assured.

1

The Changing Context for Foreign Assistance

Responding to Developing Country Aspirations for Effectively Using S&T

SHARED BENEFITS FROM THE APPLICATION OF SCIENCE AND TECHNOLOGY

Each year tens of millions of children die because of lack of access to adequate health care, food supplies, and clean water. The death rates from HIV/AIDS, tuberculosis, malaria, and other widespread diseases continue their upward trajectories. Life-sustaining ecosystems throughout the developing world are being damaged beyond repair in quests by both the rich and the poor for immediate utilization of natural resources.

Despite the efforts of many developing-country governments and local institutions—supported by international organizations, bilateral donors, and private organizations—to moderate these and other life-threatening problems, more than 100 developing countries face ominous long-term development issues that adversely affect vulnerable populations with unrelenting intensity. At the same time, tens of millions of lives are plunged deeper into poverty each year as the result of natural disasters and armed violence that strike throughout the developing world, an example of which is

> **BOX 1-1**
>
> I've been in war, and I've been through a number of hurricanes, tornadoes, and other relief operations; but I have never seen anything like this. Millions are homeless, and the international community has pledged $2 billion in relief efforts.
>
> SOURCE: Former Secretary of State Colin Powell as he viewed damage from the tsunami that struck Indonesia and other Southeast Asia countries in January 2005. Tsunami Aid Pledges Top $3 Billion. 2005. CBS News, January 5, 2005.

TABLE 1-1 Development Indicators: Low- and Middle-Income Countries and the United States

Region	Population (millions)	Life Expectancy (years)	GNI per Capita	% Population below $1 Poverty Line*	R&D Expenditures % of GDP	Fixed Line/Mobile Subscribers ß (per 1000 people)	Net Aid Flows ($ millions)
East Asia & Pacific	1,855	70	1,070	14.9	1.11	357	7,131
Europe & Central Asia•	472	68	2,580	3.6	.9	438	10,465
Latin America & Caribbean	533	71	3,280	9.5	.53	416	6,151
Middle East & N. Africa	312	69	2,390	2.4	--	237	7,629
South Asia	1,425	63	510	31.3	.75	61	6,171
Sub-Saharan Africa	705	46	500	46.4	--	62	24,146
United States ß	296	78	41,400++	--	2.79	1117.9	--

Key Indicators: Regional Data from the WDI Database http://www.worldbank.org/data/databytopic/reg_wdi.pdf
* World Development Indicators 2005 (World Bank): Poverty http://www.worldbank.org/data/wdi2005/pdfs/Table2_5.pdf
ß CIA World Fact Book http://www.cia.gov/cia/publications/factbook/geos/us.html
\+ Fixed Line and Mobile Phone Subscribers http://-.T://graphwww.nationmaster.com med_pho_sub
++ United States GNI per Capita: http://www.worldbank.org/data/databytopic/GNIPC.pdf
• Europe & Central Asia: Albania, Armenia, Azerbaijan, Belarus, Bosnia and Herzegovina, Bulgaria, Croatia, Czech Republic, Estonia , Georgia, Hungary, Kazakhstan, Kyrgyz Republic, Latvia, Lithuania, Macedonia FYR, Moldova, Poland, Romania, Russian Federation, Serbia and Montenegro, Slovak Republic, Tajikistan, Turkey, Turkmenistan

BOX 1-2
The Role of the U.S. Agency for International Development (USAID)

USAID is an independent government agency that provides economic, development, and humanitarian assistance in 100 developing countries. The types of assistance include technical assistance and capacity building, training and scholarships, food aid and disaster relief, infrastructure construction, small-enterprise loans, budget support, enterprise funds, and credit guarantees. USAID has partnerships with American businesses, private voluntary organizations, indigenous groups, universities, international organizations, other governments, trade and professional associations, faith-based organizations, and other U.S. government agencies. USAID has working relationships through contracts and grant agreements with more than 3,500 companies and over 300 U.S.-based private voluntary organizations. Its budget for FY 2005 was $9 billion, of which $3.7 billion was managed jointly by USAID and the Department of State, and $1.1 billion was PL-480 Food for Peace.

SOURCE: USAID Primer: What We Do and How We Do It. Washington, DC: USAID, November 2005.

indicated in Box 1-1. On a broader scale, Table 1-1 indicates the economic gap between industrialized and developing countries.

Science and technology (S&T) capabilities are fundamental for overcoming many types of problems in developing countries; for example, in the health sector, scientific research supported by the U.S. Agency for International Development (USAID) led to the development and introduction of oral rehydration therapy, which became the cornerstone of international efforts to control diarrheal diseases. The agency carried out research that established that two cents worth of vitamin A given to individual children every six months could reduce child mortality in many countries by over one-third.[1]

USAID's mandate is very broad, of course, and its portfolio extends well beyond health, as indicated in Box 1-2. Many other development organizations have also financed research and innovation activities in almost all development sectors. In addition, multinational companies, private foundations, and international research centers have supported such activities in developing countries.

---

[1]USAID. Report to Congress on Health-Related Research and Development Activities at USAID. Washington, DC: USAID, June 2005.

There is a growing consensus among development specialists that research and innovation are critical elements of the international effort to address difficult development issues within the much broader challenge of effectively applying S&T to address problems in many types of physical, political, and economic environments.

Problems in developing countries affect the United States in many ways; for example, emerging and endemic diseases, such as SARS, avian flu, and tuberculosis, cross borders at unprecedented rates as international flows of people and goods increase. Environmental threats—including regional air pollution, growing water scarcity, and dwindling biodiversity—affect local livelihoods as well as U.S. interests and the interests of many other nations.

As to direct U.S. benefits from S&T-based foreign assistance activities, modern technologies deployed in distant countries from vaccines to information systems can be important in limiting the extent that problems in these countries adversely affect both local populations and the broader global community. In addition, the talents and perspectives of geoscientists, biologists, and other researchers in poor countries contribute to international science. Unique innovations by local engineers and researchers to cope with problems prevalent in harsh environments often lead to broader replication such as the use of ferro-cement and new approaches to dry-land agriculture.

Meanwhile, global trade is expanding, along with international integration of financial systems and growth of worldwide communication networks. However, many developing countries lack both the financial resources and the technical skills and experience to participate effectively in this globalization dynamic. Indeed, some are becoming victims of the process as global markets become more competitive, and longstanding trade patterns are disrupted. Many governments are uncertain about the new requirements of the World Trade Organization (WTO) and are deeply concerned that they will be isolated further from the mainstream of international commerce. How will they cope with strict enforcement of intellectual property rights, demands for higher levels of quality control of export products, and other legal obligations, they ask.

BOX 1-3

USAID has helped put Bangladesh's number two export, shrimp, on a much firmer footing in the international market place by launching the Seal of Quality Program. Since exporters must respond to emerging global standards in food safety to receive the seal, the program helps ensure the long-term viability of exports currently valued at over $300 million annually.

SOURCE: NRC report of field visit to Bangladesh, January 2005.

WTO is, nevertheless, a reality. Few countries have a choice other than to attempt to adjust their trade and related policies even if newly established international norms and standards adversely affect their economies. These adjustments in developing countries in turn often directly affect American consumers and American businesses. Box 1-3 sets forth an example of a USAID project in Bangladesh that has important implications for enhancing capabilities to meet current standards for international trade. A call for assistance related to international trade from the USAID mission in Bolivia is presented in Box 1-4. The situation there in 2004 exemplified the international uncertainty associated with the evolving trade environment.

S&T, even when narrowly defined, are integral components of U.S. foreign policy and U.S. international programs—particularly foreign assistance activities. The United States benefits on many fronts from successful foreign assistance programs. These programs are now widely recognized in Washington as essential activities in promoting the national security interests of the United States.[2]

Foreign assistance, probably more than any other international endeavor, provides opportunities for the U.S. government and its partners to join on a continuing basis with political and economic leaders, intellectuals, and activists of dozens of countries in constructive dialogues and in concrete projects designed to enhance the quality of life of hundreds of millions of people. S&T are often the keystones for successful projects and therefore focal points for discussion and analysis.

In sum, the developing countries have urgent needs to use international S&T achievements effectively while the United States has innumerable opportunities for promoting humanitarian, political, economic, and national security interests through sharing its expertise in S&T. These mutually beneficial challenges pro-

---

BOX 1-4

Guidance on how USAID can most effectively use international trade negotiations and agreements to mutually support S&T developments in the United States as well as in host countries would be valuable. USAID has provided assistance on trade capacity building in a number of countries, including Bolivia. This assistance is directed to enhancing a country's capability to participate effectively in trade negotiations, including expansion of civil society participation in the process, provision of training for officials on important trade topics, and technical assistance to private enterprises that are or could be involved in international trade.

SOURCE: USAID Bolivia, December 2004.

---

[2]The White House, National Security Strategy of the United States of America. Washington, DC, September 2002.

vide the backdrop for this report on the role of S&T in foreign assistance. Maintaining and strengthening the contributions of the science, engineering, and medical capabilities of the United States to programs administered by USAID are the themes of the report. These contributions result in improved selection of assistance interventions, better-designed programs, more rigorous evaluations of the effectiveness of interventions, and broader applications of S&T.

SCIENCE AND TECHNOLOGY AS A
BROAD PLATFORM FOR DEVELOPMENT

The interim report[3] of this study released in October 2004 defined the term "science and technology" (S&T) as used throughout the study to include the natural sciences, engineering, technology, the health sciences, and the economic and social sciences. This report continues to include these disciplines within the scope of S&T. In most cases in the developing countries, S&T activities are components, or enabling elements, within programs directed to achieve educational, economic, social, and political objectives. This concept recognizes the pervasive role of S&T in development and is somewhat broader than more traditional definitions of S&T, which focus on research and science and engineering education.

From the vantage point of developing countries, S&T should involve interconnected national and international systems of activities that encourage the acquisition and generation of important knowledge and the application of this knowledge to improve the quality of life and the security of populations. Thus, S&T are fundamental building blocks for development.

In the context of U.S. foreign assistance, S&T are integral to the capacity of the public and private sectors in developing countries to:

• Provide technical services that support economic and social development—such as provision of health care, education, agriculture extension, transportation, communications, maintenance and upgrading of water supplies and sanitation facilities, management of natural resources, and energy and environmental services;

• Assess the technical and economic merits of technologies being considered for use in the country of interest and within that context carry out research, development, technology transfer, technology adaptation, and technology application activities;

• Produce industrial goods and agricultural products based on technologies and modern management methods that are well suited to the local environment;

---

[3]National Research Council. Science and Technology in U.S. Foreign Assistance: Interim Report to the Administrator, U.S. Agency for International Development. Washington, DC: The National Academies Press, 2004.

• Prepare and evaluate implementation of economic, trade, industrial, agricultural, health, education, environmental, and other policies that have technical dimensions or that influence the acquisition and use of technical resources;
• Participate in international trade negotiations, environmental treaty discussions, and other types of policy dialogues involving technical issues of political, economic, and social importance;
• Conduct programs that heighten public awareness of the potential and limitations of modern technologies to improve the well-being of the public; and
• Develop an appropriate physical infrastructure, human resource base, and educational and training institutions to support the foregoing activities.

Box 1-5 highlights concerns over inadequate attention to S&T in Mali where USAID has major programs but invests little in developing human resources trained in important S&T fields.

In addressing the role of USAID in capitalizing on the S&T strengths of U.S. and other organizations, this report gives special attention to the agency's capabilities to:

BOX 1-5

As a result of Mali's heavy dependence on agriculture, combined with a relatively inhospitable and increasingly fragile environment, Mali's stability is directly linked to natural systems. It is essential to devote greater attention to how S&T resources can be used to sustain livelihoods without substantially degrading the natural resource base.

SOURCE: Unpublished report of the NRC Committee on Science and Technology in Foreign Assistance on field visit to Mali, March 2005.

• Assess the S&T capacity of developing countries to design, manage, and evaluate programs that contribute to the development and maintenance of this capacity;
• Evaluate available technologies and encourage development of promising new approaches while incorporating suitable technologies, research findings, and modern management methods in USAID projects—with special attention to facilitating the transfer of these methods and technologies to the developing countries themselves;
• Participate effectively in interagency and international discussions involving S&T-related issues in developing countries while supporting and helping to coordinate U.S. government-wide S&T activities relevant to USAID's development objectives; and
• Recruit, retain, and effectively utilize personnel capable of supporting the foregoing activities.

USAID has valuable experience with each of these activities. Indeed, the agency has a long history of international leadership in mobilizing technical exper-

BOX 1-6

The International Center for Diarrheal Disease Research in Bangladesh was established in 1978 with major support from USAID. It has had stunning success in developing treatments for these diseases, and its hospital in Dhaka now saves the lives of more than 30 children per day while spreading the results of its research and its experience in treating patients to tens of millions of children throughout South Asia. The center has been renamed the Center for Health and Population Research, reflecting its expansion to include hospital management, epidemiology, family planning, and child survival.

SOURCE: Report of the NRC field visit to Bangladesh, January 2005.

tise and related resources to promote development. Since the 1960s, USAID has been in the forefront among development agencies in institution building—for example, in supporting the establishment of high-quality technical universities; hospitals, clinics, and medical research centers; agricultural research and extension organizations; and environmental agencies and regulatory structures. While USAID's interest in institution building has been on the decline in recent years, the committee nevertheless was able to draw on extensive experience of the agency in formulating its views as to future directions for institution building as well as other activities. Box 1-6 highlights one of USAID's long-standing institution-building programs in Bangladesh.

This report emphasizes the importance of considering S&T within a broad systems context that determines the effectiveness of the use of technologies in specific development sectors. At the same time, support of research and innovation, which are core aspects of more traditional definitions of S&T, should not be pushed aside; for example, Table 1-2 points out a number of important engineering challenges in the energy sector that require solutions based on research and innovation. Some of these challenges could be addressed by USAID and its partners, while others are more appropriate for the private sector. The importance of advances in this sector cannot be overstated given projected increases in the cost of energy as worldwide demand increases. Table 1-3 addresses the emerging field of nanotechnology.

PAYOFFS FROM INVESTMENTS IN S&T

A few developing countries where USAID has invested in large S&T-oriented programs (e.g., Thailand, Korea, Brazil) have demonstrated the payoff, particularly in increased labor productivity, from building an effective indigenous S&T infrastructure that enables the countries to use the technological achievements of others while gradually realizing the benefits of their own accom-

TABLE 1-2 Research and Training Challenges in Energy

Advances in wind technology are putting this technology within reach of some developing countries. Capital costs are likely to continue to drop over the next few years.

Improving the energy efficiency of transportation systems has very large economic and environmental implications.

Maintaining and upgrading conventional power plants is a challenge facing many developing countries.

Developments continue in sophisticated control systems for power transmission and distribution systems, requiring additional training and maintenance capabilities.

Hydrogen technology and fuel cells are of increasing interest in some developing countries.

The integrated gasification combined cycle (IGCC) is increasingly the technology of choice for coal utilization. There may be pressure on development assistance to "buy down" capital costs and to provide training in plant operations. IGCC is much more complicated to operate and maintain than traditional coal plants.

Some countries will export liquefied natural gas. Effective export and liquefaction facilities can be major S&T challenges.

Carbon capture and storage are important for fossil fuel systems throughout the world. Key issues include capacity to develop the legal and regulatory frameworks as well as to evaluate and monitor activities.

Reducing methane emissions from landfills, coal mines, and other fossil fuel sources is increasingly important, requiring technology transfer capabilities in developing countries.

Cleaner fuels will continue to be a priority for health as well as environmental reasons in urban areas throughout the world.

plishments.[4] The adaptation of Western S&T approaches to local circumstances has been an important factor in the economic growth of these countries. On a more limited scale, many USAID-supported projects in a large number of countries with substantial S&T components have had very positive impacts in improving economic and social conditions. At the same time, an important lesson has been the need to encourage development of an innovative private sector (see Box 1-7). Unfortunately, many developing countries, particularly the poor countries of Africa, do not have the human resources, physical and economic infrastructures, and access to capital to take full advantage of the S&T expertise and achievements of the United States and other industrialized countries.

---

[4]See, for example, D. E. Bloom and J. Williamson. Demographic transitions and economic miracles in emerging Asia. World Bank Economic Review 12(3)(1998):419-455.

TABLE 1-3 Applications of Nanotechnology Relevant to Developing Countries

Renewable energy: Improved solar cells; production and safe storage of hydrogen.
Agricultural productivity enhancement: Nanoparticles that deliver nutrients, fertilizers, and herbicides to crops and improve livestock nutrition.
Water treatment and remediation: Portable and affordable filters made from nanomaterials; specially coated nanoparticles for chemical and magnetic processes that remove hazardous pollutants.
Disease diagnosis and screening: Handheld technologies for blood diagnostics and for tests for hormone imbalances and diseases.
Drug delivery systems: Hollow capsules and specially coated spheres for drug delivery; improved shelf life using nanomaterials.
Food processing and storage: Improved plastic film coatings; sensors to detect contamination by pathogens.
Air pollution and remediation: Destruction of air pollutants and improvement in the efficiency of catalytic converters.
Construction: Less expensive and more durable housing materials, water-resistant asphalt and concrete, and self-cleaning surfaces for public facilities.
Health monitoring: Biosensors that continuously track glucose, carbon dioxide, and cholesterol levels.
Vector and pest detection and control: Specially targeted pesticides, insecticides, and insect repellents and sensors to detect pests.

SOURCE: P. Singer et al. Harnessing nanotechnology to improve global equity. Issues in Science and Technology, University of Texas at Dallas (2005):58.

BOX 1-7

There certainly are more private entities and networks that deal with S&T issues. A key issue in strengthening S&T capacity in developing countries will be how these can be tapped and how USAID can assist in these efforts.

SOURCE: USAID Colombia, November 2004.

For poor countries that cannot sustain a strong S&T infrastructure in the absence of unrealistically large external assistance programs, regional and other approaches may be appropriate for providing gateways to S&T that can contribute to improved economic and social progress. The experiences of the many regional S&T institutions that have been supported by USAID and other donors in recent years should be carefully examined to improve understanding of the cost-effectiveness and political feasibility of such approaches. USAID has extensive experience in twinning American institutions, primarily universities, with counterpart institutions in the poor countries for periods as long as 20 years; and the importance of this networking in developing human capital deserves close examination to help guide efforts to emulate successful programs. In any event, the necessity to examine how S&T institutions can best respond to development requirements and capabilities country by country is clear.

A series of recent reports document the conclusions of a number of organizations that effective use of S&T can significantly enhance the development process. These reports include the following:

• R. Watson, M. Crawford, and S. Farley. Strategic Approaches to Science and Technology in Development, Policy Research Working Paper. Washington, DC: The World Bank, April 2003.
• House of Commons. The Use of Science in UK International Development Policy. London: House of Commons Science and Technology Committee, 2004.
• The InterAcademy Council. Inventing a Better Future, A Strategy for Building Worldwide Capacities in Science and Technology. InterAcademy Council: Amsterdam: 2004.
• U.N. Millennium Project, Task Force on Science, Technology, and Innovation. Innovation: Applying Knowledge in Development. Earthscan. Sterling, VA: 2005.
• Canada's International Development Research Center. Support to Science, Technology, and Knowledge for Development: A Snapshot of the Global Landscape. Canada's International Development Research Center with the World Bank and the Rockefeller Foundation, 2005.

The reports argue that investments is S&T in developing countries, if appropriately targeted and sustained, can provide substantial benefit to local populations. Quantifying the cost-benefit ratio of investments in S&T in developing countries, however, has not been done in these reports or elsewhere. Studies of the impact of foreign assistance projects dependent on engineering skills have shown positive results. Efforts to correlate investments in basic research with economic growth have been plagued by methodological problems that are amplified in developing countries where basic standard-of-living improvements are often the most important outcome of such investments.[5] Still, the numerous examples of the impacts of S&T investments cited in this report and in the reports

---

[5]See, for example, M. Clemens, S. Radelet, and R. Bhavnari. Counting Chickens When They Hatch: The Short Term Effect of Aid on Growth. Working Paper No. 44. Washington, DC: Center for Global Development, revised Nov. 2004; and A. J. Salter and B. R. Martin. The economic benefits of publicly funded basic research: A critical review. Research Policy 30(2001):509-532.

of others provide authoritative testimonials that carefully designed S&T-related programs can benefit populations in tangible ways.

Countries at all levels of development have a strong desire for more robust S&T capabilities. In the first instance, many would like to be able to use the products of decades of international research and innovation activity—whether the technology is a device to capture wind power, a genetic approach to improve plant resistance to pests, or software to optimize chemical production processes. As to their aspirations for a self-sustaining indigenous capability to develop, adapt, and use modern technologies effectively, the type and extent of an S&T capacity that can effectively respond to development challenges vary greatly among countries that are recipients of U.S. foreign assistance. But some capability—to understand the potential and limitations of S&T, to select suitable foreign technologies, and to develop local innovations—is a continuing need in every country.

In almost all developing countries, well-trained managers are increasing in number, and new groups of specialists trained in various S&T disciplines are emerging every year. If deployed within an appropriate political, economic, and organizational framework, the skills of the managers and specialists can contribute significantly to local efforts to overcome poverty, to promote sustainable development, and to realize benefits from private investment and expanded global commerce. Too often, however, these specialists are not well integrated into the priority activities of government and business organizations or do not have access to adequately equipped facilities where they can use their talents. When their human skills are left on the sidelines, a brain drain of top talent may follow. A key to effective use of S&T in developing countries is a long-term commitment by political and economic leaders of the governments to building and using technological capabilities as cornerstones of development.

As previously noted, there are vast differences in the capabilities of the many poor African countries with only a few trained S&T specialists to use technologies effectively and the technology-skilled middle-income countries where USAID has programs. Indeed, in some African countries, significant S&T capacity probably remains decades into the future. Limited capabilities are needed now, however.

In sum, S&T capacity on its own will be of little significance in developing countries. But when effectively integrated into the mainstream of development, S&T can make significant contributions to social and economic progress. Even in the poorest countries, investments in demand-driven S&T deserve priority. And even in the most advanced developing countries, investments in supply-driven S&T may have limited returns.

The importance of technology in development is illustrated in the December 2004 conclusions of the National Intelligence Council—an organization reporting to the Director of National Intelligence—after a year-long set of unclassified consultations on global trends with hundreds of experts throughout the world:

The gulf between "haves" and "have nots" may widen as the greatest benefits of globalization accrue to countries and groups that can access and adopt new technologies. Indeed, a nation's level of technological achievement generally will be defined in terms of its investment in integrating and applying the new, globally available technologies—whether the technologies are acquired through a country's own basic research or from technology leaders. Nations that remain behind in adopting technologies are likely to be those that have failed to pursue policies that support application of new technologies—such as good governance, universal education, and market reforms—and not solely because they are poor.

Those that employ such policies can leapfrog stages of development, skipping over phases that other high-tech leaders such as the United States and Europe had to traverse in order to advance. China and India are well positioned to achieve such breakthroughs. Yet, even the poorest countries will be able to leverage prolific, cheap technologies to fuel their own development—although at a slower rate.[6]

The "bottom line" of this assessment by the National Intelligence Council is highlighted in Box 1-8.

While there is wide recognition that S&T should be important components of the development process for even the poorest countries, the characteristics and extent of S&T capabilities and activities that are appropriate depend on conditions in the specific countries. The accumulated experience of American institutions over many years can help guide on a broad basis the approaches of both local governments and international partners in strengthening important elements of S&T infrastructures—approaches that usually call for significant adaptation of American concepts.

> **BOX 1-8**
>
> To adaptive nations go technology's spoils.
>
> ---
>
> SOURCE: U.S. National Intelligence Council. Mapping the Global Future, Report of the National Intelligence Council's 2020 Project, 2004.

THE CHANGING GLOBAL ENVIRONMENT AND APPROACHES TO FOREIGN ASSISTANCE

Approaches to foreign assistance by different bilateral donors and international organizations vary greatly. Many are in a state of change in response to new global challenges, but several trends relevant to this study are clear.

---

[6]National Intelligence Council. Mapping the Global Future, Report of the National Intelligence Council's 2020 Project. Washington, DC: National Intelligence Council, December 2004.

• Global programs rooted in S&T to combat infectious diseases, expand food supplies, and protect the environment, for example, are growing in number and size.

• Some donors are moving toward providing budgetary support for activities in broadly defined areas of development. However, USAID continues to emphasize support of specific projects with well-defined boundaries and objectives in order to ensure that the agency does not fuel corruption.

• Foreign assistance activities are increasingly intertwined with counter-terrorism efforts involving a number of national and international institutions active in foreign assistance activities, as exemplified by the situation in the Philippines described in Box 1-9.

• Development agencies are giving greater attention to private sector development, which may lead to more emphasis on supporting engineering capacity and less attention to support of public sector research capacity.

• Local civil society organizations are playing an increasingly important role in the implementation of foreign assistance programs, but few have strong S&T capabilities.

• Africa, where many countries are plagued by economic stagnation, has emerged as a priority geographic area for assistance, as reflected in agreements at the G-8 Summit in Gleneagles, Scotland, in 2005.

• The information revolution is having a dramatic effect on the design and implementation of assistance programs in almost all sectors.

Many additional developments are particularly important for USAID, including the following:

• While USAID has lost much of its capability to manage large-scale nation-building programs, it must now recover such capabilities to address high-priority problems in Iraq and Afghanistan and possibly elsewhere, particularly in the fields of engineering, economics, and political science.

• While some developing countries increasingly rely on modern manufacturing, information, and communications technologies to fuel economic development, USAID does not support the transfer of such technologies if they will be used to manufacture products or provide services that compete with products or services offered by American companies.

• USAID's poverty alleviation efforts seem concentrated in Africa, but some Asian countries with greater S&T capacities for supporting these efforts, such as Pakistan, deserve continuing support.

As the levels of assistance funding continue to increase and as programs expand in many directions, coordination of activities among the donor governments is increasingly important and complex. Coordination of S&T-related activities is particularly critical given the limited capabilities of developing countries to assess different approaches that may be advocated by different donors and

---

BOX 1-9

Many of the new directions of the USAID program have been determined by the strategic context of addressing global terrorism. Since September 11, many of USAID's resources have been directed toward Mindanao in an attempt to address conflict more comprehensively. This includes decentralizing the healthcare system; reintegrating thousands of rebel soldiers into a peaceful economy; helping hundreds of communities take control over their forests, fish, and water; and completing the power sector reform. Dealing with so many different problems at once is clearly a challenge, but finally gives greater recognition to the interrelationship of poverty and conflict.

SOURCE: Report of field visit to the Philippines, November 2004.

---

their international and local partners. In most countries there are a limited number of adequately trained local collaborators who have both the technical and the management skills to direct international programs. In the absence of effective coordination, overloading the absorptive capacity of important local collaborators can easily occur with the possibility of wasting resources due to inadequate management attention.

Coordination should be carried out within the context of the priorities of the developing countries themselves, and the host governments should be at the center of coordination discussions. To the extent possible, these discussions should consider all relevant programs of the many international organizations, philanthropic organizations, and nongovernmental organizations involved in providing assistance at the country level. A particularly important challenge for USAID is to find its appropriate role among the expanding network of dozens of foreign assistance providers.

Private financial flows with S&T dimensions are of growing significance; for example, more important than in the past are foreign direct investment by technology-oriented companies, remittances to developing countries sent home by émigrés to support technical education opportunities for family and friends, business and other arrangements between diasporas in industrial countries and colleagues in their countries of origin, and initiatives by multinational companies together with local partners that protect the environment or otherwise benefit local populations. Private foundations sometimes support high-risk research projects in search of breakthroughs; Table 1-4 highlights a recent initiative of the Bill & Melinda Gates Foundation in addressing critical health problems.

The role of public-private partnerships in mobilizing financial and technological resources has moved up on the agendas of a number of development

TABLE 1-4 The Bill & Melinda Gates Foundation's Grand Challenges to Global Health

Long-Term Goal to Improve Health in the Developing World	Associated Grand Challenges
Improve childhood vaccines	• Create effective single-dose vaccines • Prepare vaccines that do not require refrigeration • Develop needle-free vaccine delivery systems
Create new vaccines	• Devise testing systems for new vaccines • Design antigens for protective immunity • Learn about immunological response
Control insects that transmit agents of disease	• Develop genetic strategy to control insects • Develop chemical strategy to control insects
Improve nutrition to promote health	• Create a nutrient-rich staple plant series
Improve drug treatment of infectious diseases	• Find drugs and delivery systems to limit drug resistance
Cure latent and chronic infection	• Create therapies that can cure latent infection • Create immunological methods to cure latent infection
Measure health status accurately and economically in developing countries	• Develop technologies to assess population health • Develop versatile diagnostic tools

SOURCE: Gates Foundation, August 2005.

organizations. Of considerable interest are the activities of the Global Alliance Office of USAID. This office has sponsored more than 300 public-private alliances. Many alliances draw on the technological capabilities of private sector partners. Box 1-10 describes a collaborative effort that USAID considers successful.

In 2000 the governments of the world banded together under the United Nations umbrella and agreed to address some of the most critical development

---

BOX 1-10

Ugandan university students will receive training in computer networks and high-tech manufacturing through a partnership involving USAID, the Ugandan Government, Cisco Systems, and Electronic Data Systems. Cisco is providing $8 million and USAID $2 million to create 10 network academies in the Uganda university system. EDS will provide $4.2 million and USAID $100,000 to train Ugandan students in computerized manufacturing, with the goal of making Uganda a high-tech engineering and manufacturing hub in East Africa.

SOURCE: USAID website, June 2005.

---

problems. They identified the following eight Millennium Development Goals and established targets for meeting these goals:

1. Eradicate extreme poverty and hunger;
2. Achieve universal primary education;
3. Promote gender equality and empower women;
4. Reduce child mortality;
5. Improve maternal health;
6. Combat HIV/AIDS, malaria, and other diseases;
7. Ensure environmental sustainability; and
8. Develop a global partnership for development.

Alleviating the most abject manifestations of poverty reflected in these goals became an important objective of many foreign assistance programs. As indicated in Box 1-11, S&T have been recognized as critical components of efforts to meet these goals.

BOX 1-11

To help drive economic development and to enable developing countries to forge solutions to their own problems, a significantly increased global effort is required to support research and development to address the special needs of the poor in the areas of health, agriculture, natural resources and environmental management, energy, and climate.

SOURCE: K. Annan. In Larger Freedom: Towards Development, Security and Human Rights for All. New York, NY: UN, March 21, 2005.

Three objectives should continue to be at the top of the list of the international development agenda, namely, reducing poverty; building local capacity to stimulate and support economic and social progress while absorbing the shocks of natural and human-induced disasters; and enabling developing countries to adjust to globalization. For countries to achieve success in each of these areas, access to S&T together with the development of human capital can and must play a key role. Without continuing access to some level of S&T, no country will be able to reach a level of development that fulfills the most basic aspirations of its people.

EXPANSION OF ASSISTANCE-RELATED ACTIVITIES WITHIN THE U.S. GOVERNMENT

The responsibilities of the U.S. government for programs in developing countries are rapidly expanding and diffusing among 40 departments and agencies, with USAID now financing only about 50 percent of the government's international development programs. The independent Millennium Challenge Corporation (MCC) has a multibillion-dollar development program now directed to 23 countries although it has been slow in launching its initial projects. The Department of State has relatively new responsibilities for programs directed to combating HIV/AIDS, also with an annual budget in the billions of dollars, and its program is moving forward very quickly. A number of other U.S. departments and agencies, international organizations, and private foundations finance directly related activities as indicated in Figure 1-1.

A new office in the Department of State is responsible for planning and coordinating reconstruction activities following hostilities in countries around the globe. In addition to USAID, the Department of Defense continues to be a major contributor to reconstruction efforts in war-torn countries and plays a critical role in responding to humanitarian disasters. Many other departments and agencies, including the Centers for Disease Control and Prevention, Department of Agriculture, Environmental Protection Agency (EPA), and Department of Energy, for example, have expanded the international dimensions of their mission activities that overlap with traditional development activities. A large fraction of these programs have substantial S&T components.

USAID'S ROLE IN SUPPORTING S&T WITHIN FOREIGN ASSISTANCE

Within this myriad of expanding activities, USAID has unique and broad legislative authority for bilateral foreign assistance programs, but its role in carrying out this authority is increasingly determined by congressional earmarks and White House initiatives. As indicated in Table 1-5, many of these special programs are based in large measure on S&T.

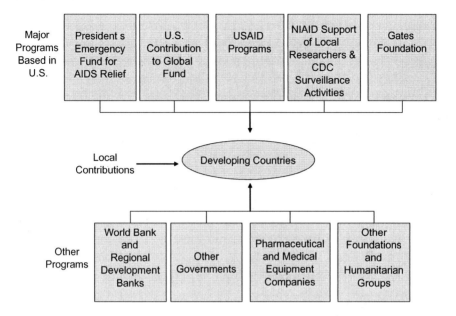

FIGURE 1-1   Organizations involved in combating HIV/AIDS in developing countries.

Earmarks and initiatives will undoubtedly continue to play an important role in determining the priorities for USAID and, indeed, in sustaining important programs. For example, earmarks in human reproduction, child health, and population have helped to maintain a balance in the overall health portfolio increasingly focused on HIV/AIDS. Nevertheless, some earmarks may be low-payoff distractions. USAID should ensure that all earmarked programs are subjected to external evaluation, along with other USAID-supported programs, to assess whether they are contributing effectively to foreign assistance objectives. When the special interest programs prove not to be cost-effective or support only narrow and relatively insignificant objectives, the White House and Congress should be informed promptly (see Box 1-12).

Since S&T are integral components of many foreign assistance activities,

---

BOX 1-12

In carrying out the mandate of a congressional earmark, the NGOs financed by USAID are primarily concerned with biological conservation and do a reasonable job in that regard. However, there is little thought given to building local capacity. When this does occur, it appears to be incidental to other objectives.

SOURCE: Report of the NRC field visit to Central America, January 2005.

TABLE 1-5 Examples of Earmarks and Special Initiatives

Examples of USAID Earmarks (2005 appropriations in millions of dollars)	Presidential Initiatives	Administration Initiatives
• $194 trade capacity building	• African Education Initiative	• Broader Middle East and North Africa Initiative
• $300 basic education	• Anti-Trafficking in Persons	• Initiative to End Hunger in Africa
• $200 microenterprise development	• Centers for Excellence in Teacher Training	• Middle East Partnership Initiative
• $165 biodiversity programs	• Digital Freedom Initiative	• Trade for African Development and Enterprise
• $100 drinking water supply	• Emergency Plan for AIDS Relief	
• $180 clean energy and other climate change policies and programs	• Initiative Against Illegal Logging	
• $1 International Real Property Foundation	• Volunteers for Prosperity	
• $4 International Fertilizer Development Center		

SOURCE: USAID, May 2005.

consideration of USAID's efforts to draw on the nation's S&T capabilities in carrying out its programs must begin with consideration of USAID's broader role in foreign assistance. To this end, the committee considered the three models set forth below that could define USAID's role during the next few years, particularly with regard to development assistance. The committee recognized that programs to provide humanitarian assistance, disaster relief, and reconstruction in war-torn regions might require somewhat different models that emphasize greater flexibility and more rapid deployment.

1. USAID could focus narrowly on several development issues—perhaps health, agriculture, and education—and develop strong internal expertise and a wide range of specialized external resources required to assist host governments develop the capability to design, implement, and manage all aspects of development interventions in these fields.

2. USAID could return to its role of decades past as a provider of S&T support across the multiple dimensions of foreign assistance that are likely to be required by low-income countries. It would support a wide array of long-term programs to build institutional capacity in developing countries, relying on greatly expanded internal technical staff capabilities to provide leadership in defining and implementing institutional development programs in many fields.

3. USAID could continue its current course of being a program management agency, responding to problems that emerge in many fields of interest to the developing countries, the Congress, and the Administration. It would use a combination of internal staffs of direct-hire specialists, assignees from other U.S. agencies, and contractor personnel to develop strategies and manage programs that are implemented by USAID's partners.

In considering these options, the committee took into account:

• The organizational structure and programs currently in place and the likelihood they will continue throughout this Administration;
• The earmarks and White House initiatives that range over many topics as noted above;
• The steady decline in USAID's internal technical capabilities and the ceilings on direct-hire staff and other personnel embedded in the agency;
• The recent decline in long-term institution-building programs financed by the agency; and
• The unique capabilities of USAID to provide field perspectives on development issues.

In addition, the decisions of the Administration to establish an independent MCC and to assign major responsibilities for HIV/AIDS to the Department of State rather than entrusting these two initiatives to USAID have eroded the agency's stature as the nation's preeminent foreign assistance provider, thereby complicating recruitment and retention of high-quality foreign assistance practitioners with S&T expertise.

The committee believes that a modification of the third option is the most realistic vision during the next several years for improving USAID's capabilities to contribute to the nation's foreign assistance effort while drawing on appropriate S&T resources in achieving its goal. USAID will, of course, continue to follow the decisions of the Administration and Congress to support program activities in many fields within USAID's established program framework of governance and humanitarian assistance, reconstruction in war-torn areas, global health, and broadly defined economic growth. However, the agency should to the extent possible select a few niche areas within this framework where it could concentrate resources and be an international leader as it has become in its support for democratic governance. Criteria for selecting areas of emphasis should include (1) high levels of developing country interest, (2) opportunities to have significant impacts on development, (3) relevance of USAID's unique field experience, and (4) limited interest of other U.S. departments and agencies in providing substantial financial support for activities in the area.

Programs in some or all of the areas will undoubtedly require substantial S&T inputs. One example of a possible area of emphasis is health delivery systems, an area the committee strongly supports. Other examples the committee believes should be considered are small innovative firms, natural resource management, agriculture extension, and information technology. Each of these areas reflects the criteria set forth above. The program emphasis within each niche area should be institution building, including establishment of research, education, training, and service capabilities. This report calls for support of schools of public health to do just that, as discussed in Chapter 3.

In order to continue to support its current portfolio of programs as well as new activities in the areas of emphasis, USAID needs stronger in-house technical staff capabilities. As recommended in Chapter 4, the agency should recruit an adequate number of technically trained direct-hire employees to lead the design and evaluation of institution building and innovative activities, particularly in the specific areas selected.

Within USAID's missions, the capabilities of personnel to identify opportunities for innovation and to hold their own in technical discussions with highly trained professionals from host countries and other donors have also eroded and need strengthening. Of special importance is a capability within the USAID missions to understand the development potential and limitations of programs of other U.S. departments and agencies and to provide these organizations with field perspectives that will increase their contributions to social and economic development.

WORKING BOTH AT THE FRONTIERS AND IN
THE MAINSTREAM OF S&T

USAID has recorded many successes in facilitating the use of S&T to overcome obstacles to development; for example, wheat-rice rotation schemes have dramatically increased agriculture production in Bangladesh. The development of a policy framework for energy networks has brought electrical power to thousands of remote villages in South Africa. In Namibia a USAID partnership with Microsoft and Compaq has developed effective e-government services and has enhanced civil participation in parliamentary affairs.

Biotechnology, nanotechnology, electronic technology, and other technological areas may be opening new vistas to improve life in poor countries. USAID should be fully aware of the potential and limitations of such technologies. Even more importantly, USAID should have a strong capability to draw on many proven technologies in ensuring that its investments in international development have the largest possible returns.

S&T sensitivity throughout the agency can have significant payoffs. Up-to-date awareness of S&T development is increasingly important in both stimulating and coordinating innovative activities not only within the U.S. government but also in partnership with foreign donors, multinational corporations, and international NGOs.

The effects of the erosion of USAID's technical capacity during the past two decades are evident in Washington and in the field. USAID is increasingly viewed as simply a mechanism to pass through funds to other organizations as reflected in Box 1-13. Its competence as an agency steeped in development realities but staying abreast of rapidly advancing technological opportunities is doubted by other U.S. departments and agencies in spite of its long history as an intellectual leader in many successful development enterprises.

BOX 1-13

At the interagency meeting on developing an early warning system for future tsunamis all that other agencies wanted from USAID was money to enable them to buy hardware for their satellite and related systems.

SOURCE: Personal communication to committee staff from a senior USAID official, May 2005.

This characterization of USAID needs to be changed, and a strengthened S&T orientation within the agency will go a long way toward enhancing the agency's role and credibility as a leader in international development while improving the effectiveness of U.S.-supported programs.

This chapter has highlighted the potential contributions to international development of modern technologies. Some of these technologies may be within the grasp of developing countries. Others may be only long-term targets for poor nations, but there are also simple innovations that can be used effectively even in

BOX 1-14

I can't tell you the number of times our counterparts (and beneficiaries) have said that as much as they welcome our funding, they would welcome even more our ability to engage on technical matters.

USAID Kosovo, Dec. 2004.

the poorest countries (e.g., pedal driven ground water pumps, plastic bottles that measure and contain the correct amount of bleach needed to destroy bacteria in dispensers of drinking water, and concrete towers supporting electronic connections for transmitting signals of mobile telephones). As USAID intensifies its efforts to enhance the capabilities of developing countries to use more advanced technologies, the agency must not neglect the incremental improvements that can be realized through wider use of technologies that have been available for many years.

The importance of USAID's field experience in helping to ensure that U.S. assistance efforts involving S&T are sound and have impact cannot be overstated. A report from USAID Kosovo, highlighted in Box 1-14, underscores this experience.

CAN A STRONG SCIENCE AND TECHNOLOGY PRESENCE BE SUSTAINED WITHIN USAID?

A fundamental tension has existed in the U.S. foreign assistance program since its inception, taking on increasingly virulent expression as budget pressures increased in the post-Vietnam era. The basic division has been between constituencies that embrace basic human needs, or bottom-up development, versus other constituencies that focus on technology transfer, stimulation of economic growth, and diffusion of benefits to the general population from innovative nodes in the economy and society. The 1960s and the 1970s saw tremendous swings from the latter to the former, setting the stage for another swing of the pendulum back to the latter as a result of disappointments with the results of diffuse grassroots investments of the 1970s.

In the early 1980s the USAID leadership embraced S&T as essential drivers of development while recognizing many other benefits to the United States from expanded cooperation in S&T. In the wake of the Green Revolution and the emerging technological achievements of the Asian tigers (Taiwan, Korea, Singapore, and Hong Kong), USAID was restructured and the recruitment of technically trained development practitioners expanded. A rapidly expanding budget between 1981 and 1986 facilitated an approach that could increase S&T activities substantially while still maintaining traditional U.S. leadership in child survival, nutrition, food aid, and other household interventions.

As might be predicted, less than a decade later, a new USAID leadership in the 1990s was determined to change directions and support a new variant of the grassroots approach. In the face of substantial budgetary cutbacks wherein both approaches could not be supported simultaneously, S&T capabilities rapidly declined. S&T proponents within and outside USAID, particularly land-grant universities, had simply not produced sufficient evidence in a decade to balance the claims of the basic-human-needs constituencies (with ever-shortening time horizons) that long-term investments in S&T were not justifiable. In short, in the view of many, USAID's S&T activities in the 1980s and their subsequent demise reaffirmed the fundamental split between the development groups in Washington and among larger political constituencies.

As we enter the twenty-first century, it will be difficult to persuade some foreign assistance constituencies that an approach that highlights the role of S&T in USAID programs is warranted. There are, however, constituencies that recognize that even the poor countries want to reap benefits from globalization, and they recognize that S&T must play an important role. We are clearly in another era of robust resources that are available for foreign assistance. With nearly $20 billion annually in the foreign operations budget category alone, there should now be an opportunity for a revitalized S&T effort aimed at long-term economic growth while still maintaining support for grassroots and good governance programs. Stronger health systems and expanded information dissemination capabilities should become core concerns of the very constituencies that have been reluctant to embrace S&T as a priority.

As globalization of problems, institutions, and solutions moves forward, the need for S&T capabilities tethered to activities in all development sectors is greater than ever. Thus, S&T must become integrated into the U.S. government's presence abroad on a wide front, and concretely into USAID's activities. The entire foreign assistance establishment must recognize S&T achievements as crucial enablers of development and not simply as endpoints. Just as governance has become a significant overarching rationale for much of America's global presence, so S&T must be recognized as an essential platform for transforming aspirations for better lives into durable and practical reality. Only then will the sustainability of a strong S&T component within USAID be assured.

2

Five Development Challenges

The Importance of Science and Technology

The committee, in consultation with senior officials at USAID, has chosen five challenges to illustrate the importance of S&T in enhancing international development and to suggest ways for USAID to draw on U.S. expertise and experience.

1. Improve child health and child survival;
2. Expand access to drinking water and sanitation;
3. Support agricultural research to help reduce hunger and poverty;
4. Promote microeconomic reforms to stimulate private sector growth and technological innovation; and
5. Prevent and respond to natural disasters.

In each of these areas USAID has active programs spanning a number of years. In most instances these programs depend on the application of findings from the natural and physical sciences and the use of information generated by the social sciences to help ensure effective program implementation.

CHILD HEALTH AND CHILD SURVIVAL

Approximately 11 million children under age five die each year, primarily in developing countries. Of these, some four million die in the first month of life. About 75 percent of the childhood deaths are the result of pneumonia, diarrheal diseases, malaria, neonatal pneumonia or sepsis, preterm delivery, or asphyxia at birth. These problems are exacerbated by malnutrition and the lack of safe water and sanitation.[1]

Many of these deaths could be avoided with simple interventions, such as breast feeding, oral rehydration therapy, and immunizations. World leaders have agreed that one of the Millennium Development Goals, discussed in Chapter 1, should address this problem: "Reduce by two-thirds, between 1990 and 2015, the under-five mortality rate."

History of USAID Involvement

USAID's child survival agenda has been particularly active since 1985, when Congress enacted the Child Survival Program. The initial program focused on growth monitoring, immunizations, and birth spacing. The program has added new elements in response to the increased understanding of the causes of child mortality and the development of new and proven health interventions. Since that time, USAID has obligated more than $2.5 billion to child survival programs for maternal and child immunization; prevention and treatment of respiratory infections, diarrheal diseases, and malaria; breastfeeding; and nutrition and micronutrient supplementation. In addition, it has provided limited funding for clean water and sanitation, important complements to public health interventions. Annual obligations for child survival and maternal health programs have averaged about $330 million since 2001. For fiscal year 2006 the appropriation is $360 million.

Major Accomplishments of USAID and the
Wider International Health Community

Health interventions based in large measure on science and technology led to a 50 percent reduction in mortality for children under five years old between 1960 and 2000. In 1960 one in five children died before age five. By 2002 this ratio had fallen to one in twelve. However, there are significant regional and local disparities; for example, in Sub-Saharan Africa, 175 in 1,000 children die as compared to 92 in 1,000 in South Asia, or 7 in 1,000 in the industrialized countries.[2] The rates of decline seen in the last four decades have leveled off and, in fact, mortality rates in some Sub-Saharan Africa countries have risen between 2000 and 2002.

Malaria remains an important cause of childhood deaths in Sub-Saharan Africa. The announcement of a new Administration initiative on malaria commit-

---

[1]J. Bryce, C. Boschi-Pinto, K. Shihuya, and R. E. Black. WHO estimates of the causes of death in children. Lancet 365(9465)(2005): 1147-1152.

[2]UNICEF. The State of the World's Children 2005: Childhood under Threat. New York, NY: UNICEF, December 2004.

ting $1.2 billion over five years for prevention and treatment is an important response to the problem. In October 2005, the Gates Foundation announced new grants of $260 million for development of a malaria vaccine, new drugs, and mosquito control methods.

Not only can reducing child mortality save lives, it can also help motivate parents in poor countries to limit the size of their families as they recognize the increased likelihood of their children surviving to care for them in old age. USAID has been a leader in supporting greater access to voluntary family planning services. The combination of increased child survival and greater access to family planning has slowed population increases, with fertility rates, the average number of children per woman, declining from an average of 4.97 in the period 1960-1965 to 2.79 in the period 1995-2000.

The decline in child mortality rates was accomplished largely by the use of simple, low-cost treatment and prevention tools—breast feeding; immunizations for protection against diphtheria, pertussis, and tetanus; oral rehydration therapies; and micronutrient supplements, such as vitamin A.[3] USAID has played an important role in developing and promoting many of these and other lifesaving interventions and technologies to prevent and treat childhood diseases. Most experts also cite the virtual elimination of polio as another major accomplishment. Recent reports suggest, however, that new strains, originally identified in Nigeria, have led to outbreaks in Niger and in 12 previously polio-free countries. These new outbreaks demonstrate the need for continued vigilance and surveillance, not one-time solutions, in dealing with public health issues.

Continuing Challenges

USAID and the international health community have made significant progress in reducing levels of child mortality, but progress has been difficult to sustain. A more integrated approach to child health is necessary, rather than the disease-specific interventions now being used by many international health agencies, including USAID. In addition, more attention should be given to strengthening local health systems—the healthcare delivery mechanisms and healthcare workers responsible for transferring the results of new scientific discoveries and technologies into improved health outcomes. The situation is particularly severe in Sub-Saharan Africa, where healthcare systems have been battered by the effects of HIV/AIDS. Many of these systems have lost healthcare workers to AIDS; and the demand on existing workers to provide treatment and palliative care for AIDS patients has diverted attention from primary healthcare needs, including the needs of children and pregnant women.

---

[3]USAID. Report to Congress: Child Survival and Health Programs Fund Progress Report (FY 2004). Washington, DC: USAID, 2005.

Continued implementation of proven approaches to the prevention of childhood diseases and to prenatal and neonatal health services is essential. For example, more than 30 percent of the world's children have not received basic immunizations against the six common childhood diseases. Currently more than 500,000 women worldwide die each year from complications of pregnancy and childbirth. More than 4 million newborns die and 4 million more are stillborn each year across the globe. Ninety-nine percent of these deaths occur in developing countries. In response, USAID has embarked on a major new maternal- and newborn-health initiative. The program builds on its activities in neonatal health, prevention of hemorrhaging in childbirth, and other birth-related complications.

USAID's past investments in health research, in particular those focused on reducing child mortality, have led to important improvements in public health. However, the advent of major new sources of research funding and the expansion of a number of research centers to include a focus on diseases typically found in developing countries require USAID to reexamine where its limited resources can be used most effectively. The agency's extensive experience in assessing local health conditions and in adapting health interventions to local social and cultural conditions, and its strong relations with local government agencies and research organizations, suggest that its resources should be focused primarily on helping to identify and prioritize local health needs. USAID should also support the adaptation, field testing, and implementation of improved health interventions, while assisting in strengthening local health systems as discussed in Chapter 3.

USAID has collaborated in numerous research efforts on vaccines for malaria, *Haemophilus influenzae* type B (Hib), rotavirus, and *Streptococcus pneumoniae* with other federal agencies, WHO, private pharmaceutical companies, and international research organizations. Much work has been in progress for many years. The National Institutes of Health and major foundations, such as the Gates Foundation, have begun providing significant support for vaccine development, and USAID has scaled back its research accordingly.

SAFE WATER

More than one billion people do not have access to adequate supplies of clean, safe water. More than 2.5 billion people, representing about 40 percent of the world's population, are without appropriate sanitation.[4] As a result, almost 4,000 children die every day.[5] Many more become ill from waterborne diseases, including cholera, typhoid, schistosomiasis, and diarrheal diseases.

---

[4]WHO/UNICEF. Meeting the MDG Drinking Water and Sanitation Target: A Mid-term Assessment of Progress. New York, NY: WHO/UNICEF Joint Monitoring Programme for Water Supply and Sanitation, 2004.

[5]J. Bartram, K. Lewis, R. Lenton, and A. Wright. Focusing on Improved Water and Sanitation for Health. Lancet 365(2005):810.

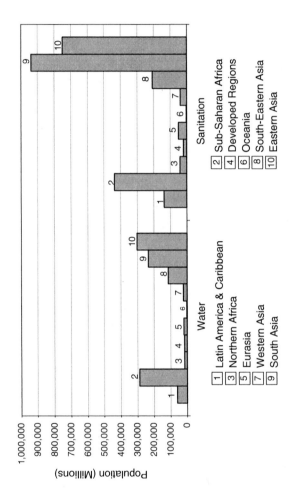

FIGURE 2-1 Population without improved water sources or sanitation by region, 2002.
SOURCE: "Water Supply and Sanitation Monitoring." World Health Organization. http://
who.int-water_sanitation health/monitoring/mp04_3pdf.

As seen in Figure 2-1, access to clean water varies dramatically. Less than 60 percent of the population in Sub-Saharan Africa has access to improved drinking water sources[6] compared to almost 90 percent in Latin America and the Caribbean and almost 100 percent in industrialized countries. Improving access to water and sanitation often depends on the deployment of conventional engineering technologies, but in other cases less costly, innovative technologies can be used, such as point-of-use treatment and storage systems, membrane technologies, household water treatment, and dry sanitation and ecological sanitation systems.

Progress to Date

Between 1990 and 2002 more than 1.1 billion people gained access to safe water, with the greatest progress in South Asia. Despite substantial gains in coverage that averaged 90 million people a year, the number of people without access to safe water has declined by only 10 million because of population growth.

During the same period, worldwide sanitation coverage increased from 49 percent to 58 percent of the world's population. However, less than 50 percent of the people living in developing countries currently have access to rudimentary sanitation. The situation is particularly severe in the informal settlements around urban areas where untreated human wastes contaminate water supplies and the environment.

At the Millennium Summit in 2000, world leaders pledged to cut the proportion of people without safe drinking water by half by 2015. At the World Summit on Sustainable Development in 2002, leaders also agreed to reduce by half the proportion without access to adequate sanitation by 2015. International aid for water supply and sanitation approached $7 billion over a recent five-year period, as seen in Figure 2-2.

History of USAID Involvement

USAID has supported drinking water and sanitation projects for more than three decades.[7] In the 1990s there was increasing emphasis on drinking water projects that could contribute to the agency's child survival programs. The agency also carried out and continues to carry out complementary projects on watershed management, coastal zone management, and industrial pollution control, all of which affect water availability and water quality. The effectiveness of these

---

[6]Improved drinking water sources—household connections, public standpipes, boreholes, protected dug wells, and protected spring and rainwater collection systems. Unimproved sources—unprotected wells and springs, rivers and ponds, vendor-provided water, and tanker truck water.

[7]USAID. Towards a Water Secure Future: USAID's Obligations in Integrated Water Resources Management for FY 2000. Washington, DC: USAID, 2001.

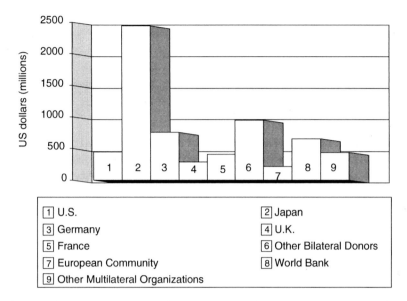

FIGURE 2-2 Average annual aid for water supply and sanitation by donor, 1996-2001. SOURCE: Gleick, Peter H. "The Millennium Development Goals for Water. http://www.pacinst.org/topics/water_and_sustainability/global_water_crisis/

projects depends on having strong internal technical staff trained in engineering, hydrology, ecology, and related areas that can develop program interventions, select appropriate contractors, and monitor program implementation.

USAID obligations for water supply, sanitation, and wastewater management were about $220 million in 2000. Of this, three-quarters was spent on projects in Egypt, the West Bank, Gaza, and Jordan. Of the $80 million obligated for drinking water supply, only $1.4 million went to support projects in Africa,[8] the region with the greatest need.

At the 2002 World Summit on Sustainable Development, the Administration announced a major new initiative, "Water for the Poor," to support the Millennium Development Goal of increasing access to water and sanitation. In 2005 USAID reported on the "success" of the initiative by noting that over 9.5 million people now have better access to water and 11.5 million people have access to adequate sanitation because of the initiative, which has provided $970 million in over 70 countries.[9] The geographic pattern of USAID obligations for water and

---

[8]Ibid, p. 5.
[9]USAID. USAID Expands Access to Clean Water with Innovative Programs. Press Release. Washington, DC: USAID, March 23, 2005.

sanitation, however, is not much different today than before the summit. In 2005 USAID reported plans to obligate about $7.7 million for drinking water projects in Africa, with an estimated $111 million for worldwide efforts. The total figure, no doubt, is a low estimate since it does not take into account any supplemental funds earmarked for restoration and reconstruction of drinking water and sanitation facilities in Afghanistan and Iraq.[10]

For more than 20 years the agency provided funds for a series of environmental health activities, including water and sanitation. The last of these programs, the Environmental Health Program (EHP), terminated in the fall of 2004 and was replaced by the Hygiene Improvement Project. One element of the EHP focused on providing environmental services—drinking water, sanitation, and waste collection—to residents of urban slum communities in India. The committee's panel that visited India was impressed with the capabilities of the Indian staff on the project and the technical backstopping provided by the USAID mission. The program seems to have been quite effective and could be a model for other programs to address the needs of slum dwellers. An important element was its focus on disseminating results and in providing information, including assessments of alternative household water treatment technologies, to NGOs and other organizations concerned with environmental health.

USAID continues to provide substantial funding for the provision of drinking water and sanitation facilities in response to natural disasters. The response to the South Asian tsunami is the most recent example. In this case a new water treatment facility was put into operation in Banda Aceh within six weeks of the disaster. The plant produces over 400,000 liters of drinking water a day, which is being distributed to thousands of people, many in refugee camps. The quality of the water is reportedly equivalent to bottled water, exceeding EPA and WHO standards.

Following Hurricane Mitch in Central America, USAID asked EPA to help with rehabilitation of drinking water treatment facilities. The program focused on enhancing the technical capacity of the water utilities and ministries of health. It included strengthening laboratory capacity, improving water treatment plants, enhancing source water protection, and training for staff responsible for managing drinking water programs. An evaluation of the program suggested that a number of short-term goals were achieved, but a longer-term effort is needed to integrate source water protection and safe drinking water components into existing local water quality programs. This longer-term view is clearly critical to ensuring an expanded availability and access to water as well as sanitation. The evaluation also highlighted the need for strong local regulatory frameworks and improvements in local technical skills. Again, both issues require long-term investments.

---

[10]USAID. USAID Investments in Drinking Water Supply Projects and Related Activities in 2005, A Report to the U.S. House and Senate Appropriations Committees. Washington, DC: USAID, March 2005.

Challenges and Opportunities for USAID

USAID has a very limited staff—less than a half-dozen personnel—with the technical skills to support its water and sanitation programs. The agency relies to a great extent on major U.S. engineering firms to design and manage its large-scale programs in the Middle East, including those in Iraq and Afghanistan. With little technical field staff, the agency's detailed knowledge of progress (and problems) on the ground is limited.

In Eastern Europe and the former Soviet Union, USAID has drawn on the skills of EPA to upgrade water treatment plants. It has also had an effective partnership with the Centers for Disease Control and Prevention to create innovative point-of-use treatment technology to provide safe water for household use. In addition, the agency created a partnership through the Global Development Alliance with Proctor and Gamble to develop another point-of-use treatment technology. These relatively inexpensive technologies provide safe water in the absence of local large-scale drinking water treatment plants.

Important members of Congress support an expansion of USAID's water and sanitation efforts. A number of advocacy groups are also encouraging Congress to earmark more substantial funding for these activities. The fiscal year 2006 appropriation includes an earmark of $200 million for drinking water supply projects and related activities. The Senator Paul Simon Water for the Poor Act of 2005 mandates access to safe water and sanitation as a policy objective of U.S. foreign assistance.[11] Highly visible water projects will continue to be a focus of congressional attention and should foster goodwill abroad.

USAID will undoubtedly continue to invest in water and sanitation facilities, with most of its funding directed to large-scale reconstruction and upgrading efforts in Iraq and Afghanistan. Access to drinking water and sanitation in other countries to complement health interventions and to support the Millennium Development Goals will also continue to interest Congress. USAID needs adequate technical staff both in the field and in headquarters to oversee these programs and to assess the numerous innovative technologies now available—for providing both drinking water and sanitation services—that can be matched to local needs, financial resources, and cultural sensitivities.

AGRICULTURAL RESEARCH TO REDUCE HUNGER AND POVERTY

For many countries, agriculture is the foundation for development. In developing countries agriculture contributes about 25 percent of the gross national product and employs about 55 percent of the labor force. Agriculture contributes to economic growth by providing food and raw materials, generating foreign

---

[11]H.R. 1973, Senator Paul Simon Water for the Poor Act of 2005.

exchange, and creating jobs on the farms and in processing and distribution. During the last 30 years, dramatic increases in agricultural productivity, largely as a result of the introduction of new varieties of rice and wheat, have expanded world food supplies. Despite these increases, however, food supplies in many parts of the developing world are inadequate.

The Food and Agriculture Organization estimates that in 2002 over 850 million people worldwide had inadequate food supplies.[12] Although this represents a slight decrease since 1996, it is far short of the goal set at the World Food Summit, where commitments were made to reduce the number of malnourished to 400 million by 2015. The problem is most serious in Sub-Saharan Africa where an estimated 33 percent of the population remains undernourished, just 1 percent less than in the period 1969-1971. By contrast, the percent of the population that was undernourished in East and South Asia declined from 43 percent of the population to 10 percent during the same period.

With expected increases in world population growth over the next half century, global food supplies must double to produce enough to meet the demand. One-half of the projected increase in demand comes from population growth, which is estimated to reach 9 billion, and the other one-half from income growth.

An estimated 75 percent of the very poor live in rural areas and depend on agriculture and natural resources for their livelihoods. Long-term reduction in poverty and prospects for sustained economic growth will depend on improvements in the productivity of rural areas. These improvements will depend on the development and application of new agricultural technologies, including those based on biotechnology, improved pest management, and better natural resource management.

History of USAID Involvement

USAID and its predecessor agencies have supported agriculture since the 1950s, initially emphasizing the transfer of U.S. agricultural technologies to poor countries, using U.S. agriculture extension services as a model. However, many U.S. technologies were not appropriate to the local needs of developing countries. In the 1960s and 1970s, USAID, other donors, and private foundations began to fund the development of more appropriate technologies and strategies.

With initial support from the Ford Foundation and the Rockefeller Foundation, the Consultative Group on International Agricultural Research (CGIAR) was established in 1971.[13] As of 2005 CGIAR supported 15 research centers.

---

[12]Food and Agriculture Organization. Assessment of the World Food Security Situation. FAO Committee on World Food Security. 31st session. May 23-26, 2005. Available at http://www.fao.org/docrep/meeting/009/J4968e/j4968e00.htm. Date accessed June 22, 2005.

[13]See http://www.cgiar.org/.

Over the years it has received $5.5 billion from the international community. The United States has been one of the largest donors, contributing almost $50 million at its highest annual level in 1986 and about $26 million in 2005.

In 1975 new provisions were added to the Foreign Assistance Act to provide program support for long-term collaborative U.S. university research on food production and distribution, storage, marketing, and consumption and for creation of the Board on International Food and Agricultural Development (BIFAD). The programs were designed to take account of the value of such programs both to U.S. agriculture and to developing nations. The university-based activities subsequently became known as the Collaborative Research Support Program (CRSP).

Currently, nine CRSP programs are funded through grants and cooperative agreements. Eight universities serve as management entities, with many additional universities participating. Leading American agricultural scientists recognize the importance of working on problems confronting the developing countries in order to broaden their scientific horizons. Many scientists are interested in participating even if they are reimbursed only for travel expenses. At the same time, the CRSP program should be driven by the interests and needs of the developing countries with the American specialists supporting these interests.

During the 1970s and 1980s, USAID also expanded support for national agricultural research systems. However, since the late 1980s funding for local research institutions has declined dramatically. Total USAID funding for agriculture has fallen from over $2 billion in 1985 to $400 million in 2003, and the current fiscal year 2006 budget request shows only $316 million in development assistance funding for all agriculture and environment activities,[14] as seen in Figure 2-3. The focus has changed from programs designed to improve smallholder incomes to increased production and processing of agricultural crops for export markets and to biodiversity conservation and management of protected areas. This decline is surprising given USAID's long history of successful agriculture programs.

The reductions in USAID support for agricultural research has paralleled reductions by other donors. Total support for the CGIAR system declined almost 2 percent a year between 1992 and 2001, and contributions are increasingly restricted to special interest programs. A long-term view of funding for agricultural research by USAID is given in Figure 2-4.

In summary, overall donor support for all agricultural programs in developing countries reached a high of about $9 billion annually in the early 1980s (at 1999 prices), falling to less than $5 billion in 1997 and under $4 billion in 2001.

---

[14]Fiscal year 2006 Sectors and Programs of Special Interest, excluding climate change activities.

The share of agriculture in overall aid budgets worldwide is now about 6 percent, considerably less than the 17 percent share reached in the early 1980s.[15]

The Millennium Challenge Corporation also offers a source of funding for agriculture-related projects and the initial compacts have included funding for irrigation, land tenure, agribusiness development, and general rural development. Furthermore, funding from the World Bank for agriculture has more than doubled in the last five years.

In part, the general decline in funding for agriculture may have resulted from increases in world food stocks and low prices in many parts of the world. The agricultural research that focused on germplasm improvement has been unpopular in some key donor countries,[16] and there has been an increasing level of concern expressed about the potential environmental effects of changes in farming systems accompanying the Green Revolution. Some of these concerns relate to loss of local control over farming systems, control that is viewed to be integral to cultural integrity. Other concerns relate to the potential for loss of control of agriculture to commercial interests, such as multinational seed and fertilizer companies. The issue of loss of genetic diversity and control over indigenous germplasm and related intellectual property is another issue frequently cited. The decline may also reflect increasing concerns in the United States and elsewhere of increased international competition from agricultural exports of developing countries.

Challenges for the International Donor Community

Continued investments in agricultural R&D are critical if world food supplies are to increase and prospects for reducing rural poverty are to improve. The global landscape for agricultural R&D has changed dramatically in the last two decades. Increasing globalization has resulted in substantial increases in trade in agricultural commodities as well as the internationalization of agricultural research. The types of institutions conducting agricultural R&D, the sources and levels of funding, and the kinds of research, technologies, and delivery systems needed now are significantly different than in the 1960s, when the international development community began to focus on agricultural S&T.

At the same time that the international donor community reduced its funding for agricultural R&D, most developing countries also reduced their support for agricultural research; for example, in Bangladesh, the Minister of Agriculture reported that the budget had declined from 22 percent to less than 3 percent of the national budget. In Mali, government funding for the agricultural research system

---

[15]Aid to Agriculture, Organization for Economic Cooperation and Development, Development Assistance Committee, Paris, December 2001.

[16]World Bank. OED Precis, The CGIAR at 31: Celebrating Its Achievements, Facing Its Challenges. Washington, DC: World Bank, Spring 2003.

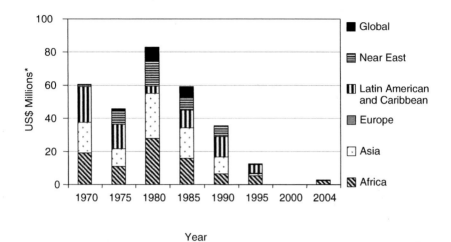

FIGURE 2-3   Estimated funding for agriculture education institutions by USAID bureau.
SOURCE: Estimates provided by Gary Alex, USAID.

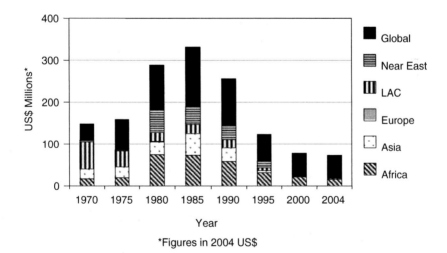

FIGURE 2-4   Estimated funding for agricultural research by USAID bureaus.
SOURCE: Estimates provided by Gary Alex, USAID.

has been slashed; and a 10-year hiring freeze has been imposed within the Ministry of Agriculture.

Despite international commitments for reducing hunger, programs of many donors in the agricultural sector, including USAID, stress exports over growing of basic food crops. In Mali, for example, scant attention is paid to dry-land small-holder farming of millet and sorghum. Rather, communities with rice or cotton potential receive the most attention. But 90 percent of the population depends on dry-land agriculture. This development is dismaying, given the link between hunger and agriculture.

Finally, USAID has been at the forefront of gender issues in agriculture. Women participate in the selection and cultivation of crops. They are marketers of agricultural products throughout Africa and in much of Latin America. They play an important role in using their income to improve health and sanitary conditions at the grassroots level.

Unique Challenges and Opportunities for USAID

As noted above, the level of USAID funding for agriculture, and particularly for agricultural research in developing country institutions, has declined substantially in recent years. At the same time, Congressional directives and earmarks have required the agency to maintain its levels of support for a number of activities, such as the CRSP programs ($28 million) and the International Fertilizer Development Center ($2 million). These earmarks combined with declining overall budgets for agriculture restrict the agency's ability to respond effectively to new opportunities; for example, there is growing recognition of the use of high-value horticultural crops in development programs. They provide essential micronutrients, they can be produced in relatively small areas, and they are a source of income for rural families. Conventional breeding and genomics are providing new varieties of vegetables and fruits with disease and insect resistance, improved nutrition, and adaptability. All of these developments are of great interest to developing nations.

The increased emphasis on short-term results has also made it difficult to provide some of the types of assistance most needed—strengthening local and regional research centers, training local scientific and technical personnel to focus on local agricultural problems, and providing extension services to farmers and others who are involved in the production, processing, and marketing of agricultural products.

In July 2004 the agency released a new agriculture strategy "Linking Producers to Markets," which focuses on the following major objectives:

• Expand trade opportunities and improve the trade capacity of producers and rural industries;

- Improve the social, economic, and environmental sustainability of agriculture;
- Mobilize science and technology and foster a capacity for innovation; and
- Strengthen agricultural training and education, outreach, and adaptive research.

The emphasis in the strategy on the role of S&T is welcome, particularly the discussion of the increasing importance of biotechnology and information and communications technologies in increasing agricultural productivity and marketing.[17]

The agency's staff with technical expertise in agriculture has declined significantly from 185 agricultural scientists and agricultural economists in 1985 to 48 in 2005.[18] As a result, mission backstopping, interactions with technical counterparts at the local level, and collaboration with important U.S.-based experts have been increasingly left to contractors. While contractors have many strengths, they often do not have the long-term commitment to the larger-scale agency objectives.

University partnerships, long the basis for USAID's agricultural efforts, have suffered as a result of a new emphasis on short-term results, the decline in long-term training and other capacity-building efforts, and the lack of effective interlocutors from USAID.

Many of the existing institutional arrangements for the provision of agricultural science and technology in developing countries have been effective, but these mechanisms should be reassessed as to their ability to meet current needs. USAID's own internal reviews of the CRSP system, in fact, have recommended such a review. Meanwhile, a long-term international effort is underway to examine the international agricultural research systems, and USAID is completing a desktop review of agriculture and natural resources management research priorities (see Appendix G).[19] The results of these reviews should be used to better focus USAID's agricultural S&T investments and to ensure that such investments meet the needs of client countries for providing adequate food supplies and promoting economic growth. USAID's agricultural programs should not be allowed to languish.

---

[17]USAID currently provides funding for a Collaborative Agricultural Biotechnology Initiative that is designed to develop technologies for small farmers and to support local decision-making systems to ensure the safe and effective application of these technologies.

[18]M. Taylor and J. Howard. Investing in Africa's Future, Partnership to Cut Hunger and Poverty in Africa, Resources for the Future (September 2005)

[19]International Resources Group 2005. Agriculture and Natural Resources Management Research Priorities Desktop Review. EPIQ II, IQC. Washington, DC: International Resources Group.

MICRO-ECONOMIC REFORM

The private sector (e.g., farmers, cooperatives, micro enterprises, local manufacturers, and multinational corporations) currently provides more than 90 percent of the jobs in developing countries.[20] Donor assistance to the private sector traditionally has focused on direct support to private sector enterprises and encouragement of macro-economic reforms, but improving the overall investment climate for both domestic and foreign private firms also requires micro-economic reforms. This section addresses such reforms without in any way seeking to diminish the importance of effective economic policies across a wide array of areas, including macro-economics, trade, and investment.

According to USAID, these micro-economic reforms include "improvements in regulations and other policy changes that directly impact the business and investment environment within which a firm operates. The development and enforcement of business regulations can influence the ability of firms to access credit, hire and fire employees, enforce contracts, own property, register their business, process goods through customs, meet standards, protect intellectual property, pay taxes, and carry out a myriad of other everyday activities directly affecting firm efficiency and productivity."[21]

Recent research suggests that business regulations are often the most important factors influencing decisions on locating, operating, and expanding firms.[22] Improvements in the business environment create profit opportunities by lowering transaction costs, reducing risks, and increasing competitiveness. It is then easier for firms to respond to changes in demand in both global and local markets. Firms find it easier to innovate, whether by adopting widely available technologies, adapting existing technologies to local needs and supplies, or developing new technologies—including new hardware and more efficient production and distribution processes.

Studies suggest that more than 80 percent of the variation of gross domestic product per capita across countries is accounted for by different levels of development of microeconomic fundamentals and that improvements in the business environment can have a significant positive effect on growth.[23] The World Bank's report "Doing Business in 2005: Removing Obstacles to Growth" estimates that

---

[20]World Bank. World Development Report 2005: A Better Investment Climate for Everyone. Washington, DC: World Bank, September 2004.

[21]USAID. USAID and Microeconomic Reform Project Profiles. Washington, DC: USAID, June 2004.

[22]Background paper by Michael Porter, Building the Microeconomic Foundations of Prosperity: Findings from the Microeconomic Competitiveness Index. www/isc.hbs.edu/pdf/GCR_0203_mci.pdf, accessed July 14, 2005.

[23]S. Djankov, C. McLiesh, and R. Ramalho. Regulation and Growth. Washington, DC: World Bank, March 2005.

for some countries improvements in the ease of doing business can add 2.2 percentage points to annual economic growth.

Activities of USAID and Other Donors

Over the past two decades, USAID and other donors have supported initiatives to stimulate private sector growth. The bulk of the assistance, which is estimated to be about $20 billion a year, or 26 percent of development assistance,[24] has been for infrastructure development, policy support, and technical assistance. Approximately one-third of this assistance has been directed to improvements in the investment climate. The focus of these activities has shifted since the 1980s, when the main emphasis was on macro-economic stability, reducing pricing and exchange rate controls, reforming public enterprise, and liberalizing the financial sector. As noted above, economic research by the World Bank and others showed the importance also of micro-economic and institutional reform as a means of improving the business environment and supporting global integration.

On a multilateral level, USAID has worked on micro-economic reform issues with the Organization for Economic Cooperation and Development's Development Assistance Committee, the G-8, the World Bank, and the World Economic Forum. The new OECD Network on Poverty Reduction is central to these activities and provides an effective forum for coordinating donor efforts.

At the 2004 G-8 Summit, government leaders agreed on actions to promote private sector development, including actions to improve the business climate for entrepreneurs and investors. These include working with the multilateral development banks to support coordinated country-specific action plans to address key impediments to business, and to develop pilot projects to facilitate comprehensive reform programs.

USAID is providing financial support for two benchmarking activities: the World Bank's Doing Business Project and the World Economic Forum's Global Competitive Index. The Doing Business Project reports on the costs of doing business in more than 130 countries.[25] The indicators are useful for examining where reforms are needed and for identifying where and why reforms have worked. For example, the 2005 report says that only two procedures are needed to start a business in Australia, but 19 are required in Chad. In each of the countries covered the World Economic Forum's Business Competitiveness Index evaluates the underlying microeconomic conditions: "the sophistication of the

---

[24]World Bank. World Development Report: A Better Investment Climate for Everyone. Washington, DC: World Bank and Oxford University Press, September 2004.

[25]Indicators on seven topics are presented—starting a business, hiring and firing workers, enforcing contracts, getting credit, closing a business, registering property, and protecting investors.

operating practices and strategies of companies and the quality of the micro-economic business environment."

A recent survey of USAID activities related to micro-economic reform indicates that more than 600 activities have been supported since 1990. Many programs have been in Eastern Europe and the former Soviet Union, where political and economic changes have required entirely new business models.[26] Activities have included development of tools for contract enforcement and dispute resolution, assistance in drafting labor regulations, and provision of equity financing for business.

In Latin America technical support for micro-economic reform began in the late 1980s with a program to identify and eliminate constraints on private sector investment in Bolivia. Fewer micro-economic reform activities have been carried out in Africa than in other regions, but some USAID missions are planning micro-economic activities to support expanded trade. Such regulations include the adoption of sanitary and phytosanitary standards.

Challenges and Opportunities

USAID is increasing its focus on micro-economic reform. Of course, the agency has a long history of support for economic research that could be used as the basis for many of its policy reform efforts as well as a broader understanding of development issues. In the case of micro-economic reform there is good evidence of the long-term effects of such changes on economic growth. However, continued support for such reforms will be challenging, requiring staff with economic skills to monitor activities, conduct assessments and research, and carry out evaluations.

A one-size-fits-all approach is not appropriate for micro-economic reform. Priorities must be consistent with local conditions—current regulatory costs and opportunities for improvements need to be identified. Once initial reforms have been made, they must be monitored and enforced. In addition, regulatory systems constantly need to be examined and adjusted in response to changing local and global conditions.

Recent initiatives to link increases in foreign assistance through the U.S Millennium Challenge Account and the World Bank's Fast Track Initiative to quantifiable reform targets should provide incentives for change. The availability of country-level data comparing the business climate also provides incentive for change.

USAID's ability to participate in these new opportunities is limited by the lack of technical staff and qualified contractors. The agency currently has an

---

[26]USAID. USAID and Microeconomic Reform Project Profiles. Washington, DC: USAID, June 2004.

inadequate evaluation capability and limited economic research expertise. USAID has only one specialist in Washington working on micro-economic reform issues, and missions have little capability. USAID can draw on contractor support for some activities, but there are few firms with relevant experience. In the past, USAID had a strong staff of highly qualified economists, directly linked to senior policy makers. This is no longer the case, and USAID is less able to influence economic policies that would allow S&T interventions to have a more substantial impact on long-term development.

Of particular concern is USAID's current lack of a strong evaluation capability and process for disseminating information on its micro-economic reform efforts. A study by Development Alternatives, Inc. found that the internal evaluation system collapsed in the mid-1990s.[27] Documentation on USAID private sector support activities had been lost. Being able to document and conduct analyses of micro-economic reform interventions and the results of such interventions seems essential.

NATURAL DISASTERS

The Indian Ocean tsunami dramatically demonstrated the immense vulnerability to natural disasters of millions of people in developing countries. More than 280,000 lives were lost; and millions more lost homes, family members, and their traditional sources of income. As in other cases of natural disasters, the international community responded, pledging billions of dollars for relief efforts and mounting reconstruction programs in every country affected by the disaster. The tsunami was just one recent reminder of the consequences of natural disasters on development prospects. The more recent earthquake in Pakistan is another.

An estimated 75 percent of the world's population lives in areas that have been affected at least once during the last two decades by floods, drought, hurricanes, earthquakes, or cyclones. During the same period, more than 1.5 million people were killed by such disasters. An estimated 85 percent of the population at risk live in developing countries and accounted for more than 98 percent of the deaths.

The economic losses associated with disasters are enormous—estimated at more than $650 billion annually in the 1990s compared to about $215 billion in the 1980s and $140 billion in the 1970s. A large portion of the losses occurred in developed countries, but these countries generally have systems in place to minimize loss of life (early warning systems, for example). In addition, they have access to immediate emergency and medical care as well as insurance programs to cover some property losses. In developing countries natural disasters are more

---

[27]D. Snodgrass, and J. Winkler. *Enterprise Growth Initiatives: Strategic Directions and Options.* Bethesda, MD: Development Alternatives, Inc., February 2004.

likely to result in significant casualties, economic and social development disruption, and diversion of funds from development to emergency relief and recovery programs. Statistics compiled by the World Bank show that in recent years natural disasters reduced annual gross domestic product (GDP) in Nicaragua by more than 15 percent, in Jamaica by 13 percent, and in Bangladesh by more than 5 percent. In Honduras, Hurricane Mitch caused losses of 40 percent of GDP, about three times the government's annual budget.

History of USAID Involvement

The USAID Office of Foreign Disaster Assistance (OFDA) was created in 1964 to provide a central locus for managing U.S. government foreign disaster assistance. Two major disasters in 1963—a volcanic eruption in Costa Rica and an earthquake in Skopje—prompted the creation of the new office.

Between 1964 and 1990, OFDA responded to more than 1,100 disasters. It provided more than $300 million in International Disaster Assistance (IDA) contingency funds and catalyzed almost $5 billion in other U.S. government funds. Between 1990 and 2000, OFDA provided $45 million annually in responding to almost 700 disasters. Floods were the most frequent form of disaster, followed by disasters involving civil strife and complex humanitarian emergencies. While the committee has focused on natural disasters,[28] it is important to recognize that addressing problems created by complex humanitarian emergencies is a large part of the work of OFDA. Increasingly, remote sensing, aerial photography, and other technologies are being used to help respond to such humanitarian crises. In fiscal year 2005 OFDA responded to 17 complex humanitarian emergencies in Iraq, Sudan, Liberia, Afghanistan, Angola, Democratic Republic of the Congo, Indonesia, and other countries, spending more than $240 million.

For more than 25 years S&T have played an important role in OFDA programs, as OFDA developed early warning systems, improved communications systems, and mounted disaster mitigation and response programs. In 1978 the National Academy of Sciences prepared two reports for USAID, exploring the role that S&T could play in strengthening the office's programs. One focused on general management issues and the other more specifically on the role of technology in disaster assistance programs. See Box 2-1 for selected recommendations from the report *The U.S. Government Foreign Disaster Assistance Program.* Several of these recommendations are equally applicable today.

In the late 1980s OFDA and USAID's Africa Bureau developed FEWS NET, a famine early warning system allowing for the exchange of water informa-

---

[28]Natural disasters are often rapid onset events, such as earthquakes, hurricanes, or floods but may also be creeping disasters, such as drought or famine. In many cases the impacts of such disasters are exacerbated by soil degradation and deforestation.

BOX 2-1
Strengthening USAID's Response to Disasters

1. Greater consideration should be given to operational and planning needs related to disasters that involve conflict or slow onset.

2. The development of stronger linkages between the AID/OFDA's disaster assistance program and the broader development programs at AID should be given careful consideration.

3. Greater budgetary support should be given to the disaster planning and preparedness activities of the AID/OFDA technical assistance program.

4. High priority should be given to research that will develop more valid and reliable measurements of disaster impacts of societal and international responses to these impacts.

5. The establishment of organizational mechanisms for the exchange of policy-related research information on disaster prevention, mitigation, and response should be given careful consideration at the international level.

SOURCE: National Research Council. *The U.S. Government Foreign Disaster Assistance Program.* Washington, D.C.: July, 1978.

tion and climate monitoring and reporting on hydro-meteorological developments likely to affect food supply, including cyclical droughts and flooding. In Asia, OFDA has worked with the National Oceanic and Atmospheric Administration using seasonal climate forecasts to cope with the effects of the 1997-1998 El Niño/Southern Oscillation. OFDA has supported a number of flood-monitoring programs in Asia, including community programs in Bangladesh, designed to reduce the vulnerability of people living in flood plains. OFDA has also provided funding for the U.S. Geological Survey's Volcano Disaster Assistance Program, which provides technical assistance to volcano-monitoring organizations around the world.

OFDA has been able to make effective use of relevant S&T resources not only from other U.S. government agencies but also from U.S.-based and international organizations. Increasingly OFDA has been able to draw on the resources of the Department of Defense to assist with immediate logistical support for disaster response. In addition, OFDA has special authority to expedite contracts for disaster response services.

Continuing Challenges and Opportunities

It is expected that the frequency and cost of natural disasters will increase in the coming decades—the result of environmental degradation, climate change, and population growth in cities and vulnerable coastal areas. These costs will occur not only in developing countries but also in the United States and other developed countries. The enormous economic and social costs caused by Hurricane Katrina revealed the vulnerability of U.S. coastal communities. Many rapidly growing urban areas in developing countries are similarly vulnerable to natural disasters as large proportions of the population live in unauthorized settlements in ecologically stressed areas.

In many countries disaster prevention and preparedness programs tend to lose out to other seemingly more immediate political priorities. Even within OFDA, prevention and mitigation programs receive only a very small percentage of the overall budget—about 10 percent—with most of the office's funding used for disaster response. Recent experience suggests that more attention should be paid to assisting countries in prevention and mitigation efforts. Furthermore, USAID's mainstream development activities generally do not include hazard mitigation activities even in the aftermath of a disaster. This disconnect between disaster response programs and long-term development efforts (for example, coastal zone management) deserves increased attention.

In OFDA, as in other parts of the agency, constraints on hiring technical staff are a problem. OFDA has attempted to deal with this by using a variety of mechanisms to borrow staff from other organizations. Only about 10 percent of the OFDA staff consists of direct-hire employees, which hampers the office's ability to influence other offices within the agency and to represent USAID to other organizations. This representation function is more important in the wake of Hurricane Katrina, as other organizations involved in disasters strengthen their staffs.

Crosscutting S&T Issues

Information and communications technology (ICT) is a critical crosscutting issue that affects a wide variety of programs in such areas as agriculture, health care, education, small business, democracy, and trade expansion. A recent survey of USAID missions indicates that 95 percent of the missions support some ICT activities, many associated with democracy, governance, or education programs. In a number of instances USAID also provides support for regulations governing ICT infrastructure, training of technicians, and ICT hardware. For example, in Africa, the Leland Initiative helped to establish policy and regulatory regimes and to support local Internet service providers. Working with Cisco Systems Inc., USAID has provided training for ICT technicians in more than 30 countries.

Turning to education, meeting the challenges discussed above requires specialists with strong scientific, technical, and engineering skills. For the most part, the committee focused on training at the university and graduate levels and strengthening of local and regional S&T institutions. Equally important, however, is the provision of science education at the primary and secondary levels. For many people, especially in Africa, this will be their only opportunity to become scientifically literate, begin to become independent thinkers, and learn critical problem-solving skills. These tools are essential in adjusting to changing labor markets, adapting and using modern technologies, and being effective participants in civil society. Good basic science and basic mathematics programs at the elementary and secondary school level also stimulate students to pursue careers in a variety of scientific disciplines.

Currently a large portion of USAID's education budget is allocated to primary education, but science education seems to be of little concern in these programs. One exception is a project to bring science and mathematics teachers from South Africa to the United States for leadership training. Clearly, the U.S. S&T education community could provide greater inputs to USAID's primary and secondary education programs.

3

Strengthening the Science and Technology Capacity of Developing Countries

Self-Reliance: The Key to Sustainability

The governments of many developing countries recognize the critical importance of local institutions and specialists being able to identify, adapt, and effectively use the S&T achievements of industrialized nations and to develop their own unique technologies. According to World Bank officials, requests for S&T-related assistance from such governments are on the rise.

Better application of technologies of broad international interest can improve many aspects of social and economic development—from pest-resistant crops to less wasteful food processing; from prenatal care and child health to the prevention and treatment of diseases; from reduction of environmental contaminants to purification of water; and from more reliable electricity to more efficient and affordable communication and transportation systems. Almost every area of USAID programming—including even governance and export promotion—is intertwined with the local S&T capabilities of developing countries.

Reflecting the continuing need for S&T capacity in developing countries, a USAID policy adopted in 1983 on institution building continues to have salience 22 years later. The policy was as follows:

> Key institutions in the development process are those that generate, adapt, and disseminate knowledge and technology at international, national, and local levels. Technology transfer is accomplished most effectively by those countries which have scientific establishments capable of evaluating and adapting knowledge and technologies to local conditions. The establishment of local institutions that have the capacity to tap and contribute to the world knowledge supply must therefore be a high USAID priority.[1]

---

[1] USAID. USAID Policy Paper, Institutional Development. Washington, DC: USAID, March 1983.

The specific technologies that are suitable for addressing development problems vary widely from country to country. In some cases, continued use of well-established health, agriculture, and engineering technologies may be more practical than adopting newer technologies that are increasingly used in industrialized countries. An important key to successful development is the capability of a country—through its governmental and increasingly its private sector institutions—to be able to select those technologies that can be effectively used and maintained at affordable costs.

Unfortunately the importance of developing S&T capacity may not be adequately reflected in the economic, research, and education policies and programs of the countries themselves or in projects advocated by their foreign partners. Only limited attention is often paid to policies that provide incentives for government or private sector organizations to invest in suitable technologies, that support training programs for the local purveyors and users of technologies—however advanced—and that ensure that product quality standards are met. Frequently public and private sector institutions simply purchase technologies that are promoted by foreign sales representatives or accept recommendations of international partners with little local appreciation of the effectiveness and limitations of the technologies that are acquired. However, many developing country governments are now striving to have stronger indigenous technical capacities to select and, when necessary, to adapt both local and imported technologies to help ensure they will perform adequately in the physical, economic, and social environments where they will be deployed. Experienced local researchers can often provide helpful advice during the selection process.

Turning to an area where millions of lives are repeatedly at stake each year, the need for local capabilities to effectively use technologies that help provide early warning of natural disasters and to support prompt and effective responses following a disaster is demonstrated all too often. USAID has a good record of supporting the deployment of modern technologies in response to hurricanes, earthquakes, floods, and other unpredictable events, but USAID has given less attention to improving capabilities of countries to prepare for and respond to such events once the international support teams have left the scene following an event. Two contrasting examples of responding to the challenge are set forth in Boxes 3-1 and 3-2.

BOX 3-1

USAID has played an important role in the establishment in Bangladesh of a system of monitoring levels of rivers that flood populated islands and low-lying coastal areas each year. These efforts, together with efforts of the government and other donors, have saved the lives of thousands of residents of flood-prone areas each year.

SOURCE: Unpublished report of the NRC Committee on Science and Technology in Foreign Assistance on field visit to Bangladesh, January 2005.

In another critically important area, nearly all countries recognize the importance of higher education in S&T disciplines. Unfortunately, institutions to provide such education are not yet well established in most developing countries. In addition, qualified teachers with expertise in S&T are in short supply at both the secondary school and the university levels.

As to the role of local researchers in the development process, the types of investments that are appropriate vary greatly from country to country. Small, poor countries may not be able to support their own research facilities, and regional approaches might be considered. In Africa, in particular, considerable attention has been given to regional education and research centers. More populous countries may be able to develop their own capabilities more easily. Whether the goal is a national or a regional education or research center, external donors must recognize that long-term commitments are needed to establish productive institutions. Too often donors are only interested in jump starting new education or research facilities for a few years. Then, in the absence of a long-term funding commitment, embryonic research activities that are on good trajectories are left on their own; and they may quickly collapse.

For decades USAID has made major contributions to strengthening higher education in S&T and related research capabilities of many countries. For example, USAID has drawn on the capabilities of the U.S. land grant colleges to work with counterpart institutions throughout the developing world. These efforts have had great impact when sustained over 10 years or more. In particular, training of Mexican and Brazilian plant geneticists has had excellent development payoffs in terms of developing and adapting crops that can tolerate harsh environmental conditions. In recent years, however, the investment of USAID in supporting local S&T educational institutions has declined significantly, as indicated in Box 3-3.

With a few exceptions, long-term commitments by USAID to support local institutions for a decade or more have been replaced by short-term projects of

---

BOX 3-2

While satellite technologies can greatly improve current capabilities to predict the times and directions of hurricanes, the countries of Central America that are in the paths of frequent hurricanes do not have the capability to use the products of this technology effectively despite the enormous economic stakes associated with hurricanes.

SOURCE: Unpublished report of the NRC Committee on Science and Technology in Foreign Assistance on field visit to Central America, March 2005.

BOX 3-3

The agency has cut back on scholarships, infrastructure, and commodities. We need to put some of those tools back in the kit.

SOURCE: USAID Administrator, May 2005

five years or less. Not surprisingly, there has been a related tenfold decline in the past three decades in the number of USAID-financed graduate students from developing countries at U.S. universities who focus on problems relevant to those encountered in their home countries. An example of the negative impact of this decline in support for higher education is reflected in the report from Mali in Box 3-4.

Of course, well-designed, long-term S&T training at U.S. universities is but one aspect of institution building. Once trained, newly minted researchers need adequate facilities to use their training. Unless potential users are interested in their research, the researchers may end up wasting their time. Still, customized training, in the United States or other appropriate settings, can be a powerful starting point for upgrading local capabilities over the long term. Clearly development of human resources must be at the top of the priority list if nations are to have the ability to adapt, develop, and introduce technological innovations of importance to their long-term economic viability. One cannot underestimate the significance of networks that result from U.S.-based training to the promotion of U.S. interests.

> **BOX 3-4**
>
> The decision of USAID to devote all of the education resources of its mission in Mali to primary education and neglect higher education is having a devastating effect both on the viability of the local universities that are in their early stage of development and on the influx of specialists trained abroad for leadership positions within the government.
>
> ---
>
> SOURCE: Unpublished report of the NRC Committee on Science and Technology in Foreign Assistance on field visit to Mali, March 2005.

Another approach that has received considerable attention in past decades has been the opportunity to link more advanced developing countries with other developing countries in a South-South transfer of technology. Perhaps the best example of such an approach that is currently supported by USAID is the linking of Israeli researchers with researchers in other Middle East countries. While politically motivated, this program has supported a large variety of scientifically productive relationships.

A particularly important type of linkage for some countries is the natural tie that emerges between scientists and engineers operating in the same disciplines. USAID has supported activities between chemical societies in different countries interested in addressing opportunities for marketing natural products (for example, in tropical areas). These relationships are often helpful both in identifying commercial opportunities and in ensuring that scientists in developing countries do not become isolated from their counterparts in the industrialized world and then lose interest in science.

Against this background of the importance of S&T capacity enhancement in almost all developing countries, ***USAID should reverse the decline in its support*** *for building S&T capacity within important development sectors in developing countries.* To this end, USAID should:

1. *Increase the number of USAID-sponsored participants in highly focused graduate training programs designed to develop future leaders in various S&T disciplines.* For the reasons discussed above, the opportunities for USAID-supported study at U.S. universities should be increased significantly, probably on the order of two- to threefold while recognizing that the number of students will not approach the much higher levels of the 1980s. The emphasis should be on training that can contribute directly to programs in health, agriculture, environment, energy, and other areas of priority interest to developing countries and to USAID. Visa problems, temptations for brain drain, and U.S. caution concerning the spread of terrorist networks into the United States will place limits on the extent that such training can be expanded. Nevertheless, the importance of training future S&T leaders at U.S. institutions has been repeatedly demonstrated through USAID programs. Such training should be reinvigorated using well-tested sandwich programs whereby time is divided between study in the United States and field research in the home countries and other proven approaches that focus attention of researchers on persistent problems in their home countries.

Training programs in the United States at the graduate level should be supplemented with (1) graduate training programs at well-developed regional and local institutions, (2) opportunities for participation by local specialists in Web-based distance learning programs, (3) short-term visits by local specialists to the United States for conferences and short-term training courses, and (4) broader use of training partnerships with the private sector operating in the countries of interest. Such training activities should be directly linked to the areas of priority USAID interest in the home countries of the trainees. To the extent feasible, the participants in training programs should be selected from a limited number of institutions to help strengthen both individual and institutional capabilities.

The balance between long-term training in home countries and abroad must be resolved country by country and on a programmatic basis. An important consideration is, of course, the collateral benefits of training in the United States, which usually results in alumni with strong admiration for the United States as well as increased interest of U.S. professors in dealing with issues related to international development.

2. *Increase financial support for applied research and outreach, including extension, at local institutions that can support host country priority programs of interest to USAID.* Strengthening applied research and outreach capabilities at important facilities can provide results of near-term significance, can help ensure sustainability through local efforts of USAID's projects, and can stimulate local interest in research. In addition, researchers often play important roles in governmental decisions as to the importation of technologies from abroad. Chapter 1 presents many examples of past USAID successes in supporting research and outreach in agriculture and health that are worthy of emulation. Model programs that attract the attention of researchers from throughout a country are often important in addressing nationwide issues.

USAID experience in developing important research capabilities in fields beyond health and agriculture should be examined to ascertain the ingredients of success; for example, USAID has played a significant role in developing economic and manpower research units in a number of countries, particularly within government ministries. USAID also has assisted in transforming stagnant industrial research institutes supported by governments into important centers of technological innovation (e.g., institutes in India and Guatemala). In some instances, however, short-term progress was halted as USAID terminated the programs because of a lack of near-term impacts. Documenting the futility of short-term efforts is also important.

A recently initiated USAID program to support Pakistani scientists is an example of USAID support of local S&T activities that is designed to help in building capacity. The Pakistan government provides up to $3.5 million to local S&T teams annually, and USAID provides $2 million for American collaborators and administrative support. Awards are based on an open competition, with applications subjected to peer review in both Pakistan and the United States. It is too early to assess the impact of the program, but early indications are that funds will enable important Pakistani organizations and their scientists to play stronger roles in national development (see Appendix K for a list of recent awards).

The foregoing discussion of applied research and extension has considered largely government-financed activities. Since much of the innovation occurs in the private sector, governments should have other tools to stimulate innovation (e.g., tax incentives, provision of technoparks and other suitable working areas, and training of private sector employees). As to financial incentives, governments should consider matching funds to leverage private investments in technology innovation and financial support for small technology-oriented businesses that are struggling to find market niches.

3. *Provide increased financial support for development of local capacity to deliver public health services.* Significant augmentation of existing pools of trained health professionals is urgently needed worldwide. Schools of public health that provide training and research capabilities should become cornerstones of health infrastructures. A strong social service component is an important aspect of such capabilities. In some cases, it may be possible to upgrade existing educations centers (e.g., Uganda). In other cases, new institutions are required (e.g., India). In general, the American model may be helpful in the development

---

BOX 3-5
Leadership Initiative for Public Health in East Africa

USAID proposes to partner a limited number of African institutions for public health training with U.S. counterparts to strengthen the institutional capacity of the African school to provide advanced leadership training relevant to the health needs of Africa, including epidemiology, health policy and planning, public administration, budgeting, human resource management, and field research.

SOURCE: Information provided by Association Liaison Office for University Cooperation in Development, USAID, May 2005.

---

of such educational centers, but the special needs and capabilities of individual countries are crucial considerations in the design of programs and supporting facilities. USAID is attempting to initiate such an approach in Africa, as indicated in Box 3-5. As populations grow, as diseases spread, and as the public's demand for better health services increases, this effort along with comparable new efforts in India and other countries are overdue.

4. *Assist important institutions in developing countries where USAID has programs in strengthening their information acquisition and processing capabilities and their electronic access to scientific collections.* As developing countries slowly build their S&T infrastructures, local education and research institutions should expand their databases on topics relevant to development, both to avoid unnecessary duplication of earlier research and to provide a better environment that will attract talented students to research. In addition, the ease of acquiring scientific literature available electronically, often accessible only through advanced library systems, should be upgraded. The expansion of broadband Internet systems and the increased number of specially designed databases throughout the world could, with modest investment, provide new opportunities for developing country specialists to stay abreast of international S&T advances in critical areas. Expanding international digital library access is also an important element of this approach.

USAID should arrange for American specialists skilled in database management and in the use of international databases to have short-term assignments in many of the countries where USAID has programs to help train local database managers. This low-cost approach would generate local interest in the use of international scientific resources; this would also help counterparts design affordable approaches to effective use of these resources.

There is a related need to upgrade many types of information resources— from text books to public libraries. While the recommendation in this report

TABLE 3-1 Areas of Technology Offering Promise for Further Development in Armenia.

Information technology, and particularly software development
Semiconductors, infrared detectors, and large single crystals
Laser technology and light detection and ranging (Lidar systems)
Precision electromechanical systems
Specialty agricultural products and processing
Nutraceuticals and functional foods
Specialty chemicals and specialty materials
Mineral refining
Earthquake engineering
Commercial applications of nuclear magnetic resonance
Genetic testing

SOURCE: National Research Council. *Science and Technology in Armenia: Toward a Knowledge-Based Economy*, Washington, D.C.: The National Academies Press, 2004.

focuses on scientific information, it should have collateral benefits in stimulating expanded information services in other areas as well.

5. *Sponsor expert assessments of S&T infrastructures in countries where USAID has major programs.* Such assessments of current and potential contributions of public and private S&T resources to development should be undertaken by teams of local and international specialists, particularly when qualified and objective local scientists are available. The assessments should provide important insights as to how host governments, USAID, other donors, and international organizations can effectively strengthen the infrastructures and integrate S&T resources into the mainstream of economic and social development. Economists and social scientists can play important roles in these assessments. If there is no indication of interest in such assessments by the host government or donor agencies, however, it is probably better not to launch a project, given the likelihood that the effort will raise false expectations of follow-on activities.

The scope of an assessment will depend on the country of interest. Ukraine, for example, has an extensive infrastructure, and a comprehensive assessment within the context of a single project would be very difficult. Perhaps dividing the assessment into a number of components might be feasible although different S&T activities often complement one another and the opportunity for synergism might not receive adequate attention (e.g., the contributions to nutrition of both health care and agriculture). At the other extreme, the infrastructure of Mali is quite limited; and as indicated during the committee's field visit to the country, a comprehensive assessment by an expert group would seem appropriate.

Table 3-1 presents one of the findings of a USAID-sponsored assessment of the S&T capabilities of Armenia. This particular finding was directed to advanced technologies with commercial potential while other conclusions emphasized the overall policy framework for S&T and trends in the development of the technical manpower base. The effort was carried out by an American team since it would have been difficult to include local specialists who were not already committed to their own approaches to improving the nation's S&T base.

Since the U.S. Ambassador in Yerevan requested the assessment, many organizations should have been interested in the results, and particularly USAID, the Armenian government, and the Armenian and international scientific communities. Some crosscutting observations were relevant to USAID's program interests (e.g., the undeveloped and poorly enforced regulatory infrastructure for protecting intellectual property rights, the paucity of research at the universities, and approaches to countering the brain drain). But follow-on activities have not yet materialized.

The cost of the assessment was $165,000, a small portion of USAID's annual program budget of $56 million for Armenia at the time.

•   •   •

Initial implementation of the foregoing initiatives within the framework of existing USAID programs should be possible without redirection of major budgetary resources. If the initial efforts have high impact, then each initiative could be easily expanded to begin to upgrade local S&T capacities. However, sustained investments will be possible only if host governments and the private sector are persuaded that investments in S&T can be profitable.

4

Capabilities of USAID to Use
Science and Technology Effectively

Providing Developing Countries with Technological Options

As underscored in Chapter 1, the potential economic and social returns from effectively embedding S&T within foreign assistance programs have been recognized by USAID, other donors, and international agencies for decades.

Within USAID, surges of interest in drawing on S&T capabilities of the United States in formulating and implementing the agency's portfolio of activities have been followed by declines in the support for S&T-related activities. The changing number and authority of direct-hire staff members with strong technical credentials have probably been the best barometer of the level of attention the agency has given to using S&T in its programs.

A primary reason for the recurrent declines has been the doubts of many USAID constituencies that S&T should be in favor when limited foreign assistance funds are at stake; for example, the proponents of targeting basic human needs as the USAID priority have seldom supported diversion of "their" funds for grassroots programs to support S&T capacity building, which they contend should come much later in the development process within poor countries. In addition, many U.S. officials, a large number of NGOs, and other organizations are focused on improved governance as the agency's priority; and they have little interest in embracing S&T as a competing priority. At the same time, development specialists have consistently supported three strands of USAID programming wherein S&T are deeply embedded—improved health services for developing countries, agricultural research, and the use of modern technologies in responding to natural and humanitarian disasters. But many of these practitioners too often erroneously assume that high-quality and relevant S&T capabilities will be immediately available whenever USAID decides to buy prepackaged services.

All the while, the interest of developing countries in improving access to S&T on a broad basis has been on the increase as reflected in the response of other donors and international organizations in embracing S&T as a driver of development. While the USAID leadership may at times recognize and support these initiatives, the agency is poorly equipped to respond to such new opportunities.

Given the many changes in the context and political support for S&T programs within USAID in the past, a few comments are offered on approaches toward S&T that the agency has adopted since its very beginning. This discussion should help set the stage for specific recommendations for a future when globalization will continue advancing, and a robust and sustained S&T capability within USAID will be more important than ever.

In the 1960s, during the early days of USAID, scientists, engineers, and health professionals played key roles in development assistance programs. These technical specialists were clustered both in central USAID offices of engineering, industry, health, and agriculture and in technical support offices of the regional bureaus in Washington. In the field, large USAID missions had many technical specialists on staff, while technical personnel located in regional hubs supported smaller missions. Their influence was widely reflected in the agency's lending and grant programs as they initiated projects throughout the agency, and many became internationally recognized as leading experts in their fields.

From the mid-1960s until 1980, USAID adopted a variety of organizational approaches to expand even further the engagement of the U.S. S&T communities in its programs. The Office of the Science and Technology Adviser to the President and the National Academy of Sciences played strong supporting roles in this regard. A Science Adviser was assigned to the USAID Policy and Program Coordination Bureau for several years. A Technical Assistance Bureau with strong offices for health, population, and agriculture was then established; a special S&T office was added to address other areas where S&T could play a greater role. The Research Advisory Committee guided the selection and implementation of innovative research projects. The Administrator appointed a Special Adviser for Environmental Affairs. In 1973, the Congress established the Board on International Food and Agriculture Development (BIFAD) to help expand the involvement of Land Grant Colleges in USAID programs. All the while, the USAID missions continued to have substantial staff capabilities to address technical aspects of their programs in a variety of fields, and the number of S&T-related projects of the agency continued to grow.

In recognition of the important role of S&T in foreign assistance, and taking into account the foregoing experience, the USAID Administrator in 1981 established a strong Bureau for Science and Technology. This bureau consolidated many ongoing activities while continuing to add new S&T programs. For more than a decade, this bureau raised the profile of S&T in agency activities and attracted many talented technical specialists to the agency.

In the early 1990s the office was reconstituted as the Global Bureau in recognition that other aspects of foreign assistance were also of significance throughout the agency, such as supporting the evolution of civil society in Eastern Europe, the former Soviet Union, and elsewhere. With the name change also came changes in personnel, and the cadre of talented specialists with technical expertise began to shrink. During the 1990s, the overall agency personnel ceilings declined sharply, and many technically trained employees were among those who were forced out by the agency's management in order to meet the requirements of Congress and the Administration. The Research Advisory Committee and other science-oriented organizations soon disappeared.

Shortly after the turn of the twenty-first century, a new structure of central "pillar" bureaus emerged. A Bureau for Global Health was established to respond more fully to the high priority given by the Administration and Congress to addressing a wide range of health and population issues, including HIV/AIDS, tuberculosis, malaria, voluntary family planning, and maternal and child health. A parallel Bureau for Economic Growth, Agriculture, and Trade (EGAT) assumed the responsibility of supporting innovation in fields other than health and population, and particularly agriculture, energy, natural resources management, and information and communications technology. A new Bureau for Democracy, Conflict, and Humanitarian Assistance also had considerable interest in S&T. This interest included application of technologies in anticipating and responding to natural disasters and in responding to other humanitarian emergencies. In addition, the bureau turned its attention to expanding the use of the social sciences in understanding and responding to development problems of fragile states.

In mid-2005 USAID initiated the process of establishing a new part-time position of Science and Technology Adviser to the Administrator on a part-time basis, and the agency began recruiting for the position. The decision to establish the position apparently was triggered by the appointment of a well-known agricultural scientist as Science Adviser to the Director of the U.K. Department for International Development (DFID). Perhaps, the interim report of this study, which stated that the present committee was considering a recommendation concerning an S&T adviser, also provided some stimulus. In any event, the responsibilities of the position and the activities of the office, if established, will probably evolve over a period of many months or perhaps years. The comments of the committee set forth in the report should assist in this evolution.

ERODED STAFF RESOURCES

As repeatedly mentioned, the technical capabilities of the USAID staff have steadily atrophied during the past 15 years. When the overall personnel ceilings declined during the early 1990s, USAID emphasized retention of generalists who were able to manage a variety of activities rather than employees with in-depth knowledge of specific fields. However, such in-depth expertise, both to help solve problems and to assist in anticipating problems, is essential if the full

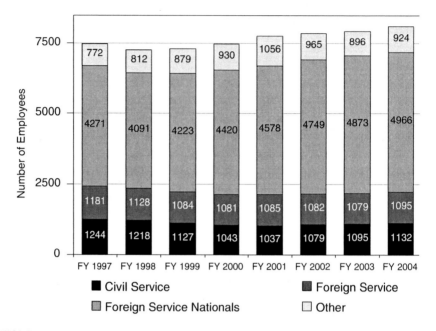

FIGURE 4-1   USAID full-time permanent employees.
SOURCE; Miklaucic, Michael. "Four Years of progress at USAID." *USAID Frontlines*
2005:6.

potential of U.S. foreign assistance is to be realized. Levels of USAID staffing
from 1997 through 2004 are presented in Figure 4-1.

Figure 4-2 indicates the number of direct-hire staff assigned to different
program areas. Many staff members do not have technical backgrounds in their
fields of responsibility; they rely primarily on experience gained on the job.

In 2005 Congress concurred with a proposal to establish 225 new limited-
term civil service positions over a three-year period. These appointments for five-
year periods are intended to reduce USAID's dependence on contractor personnel
and personnel of other government agencies who are on assignment within
USAID. Therefore, 225 positions will be eliminated from the authorized level of
personnel embedded within USAID who are employees of contractors and other
agencies.

Early indications are that a significant number of the new limited-term positions are being filled through conversion of contractor and other personnel who
are already working in the agency to direct-hire employees. Thus, both the number and the technical qualifications of personnel available to work on USAID
programs may change very little, but bringing the formerly embedded personnel
directly into the agency should enhance agency capabilities during internal dis-

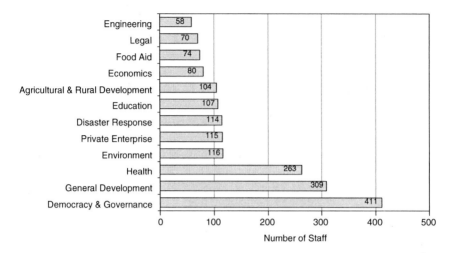

FIGURE 4-2   Assignments of USAID direct-hire program staff (worldwide). SOURCE: USAID Primer: What We Do and How We Do It. Available at http://www.usaid-ph.gov/documents/about/aidprimer.pdf. 29. Date accessed June 15, 2005.

cussions that are limited to direct-hire personnel and discussions with other agencies and other donors.

In the 1980s and 1990s USAID developed a robust program for bringing into the agency a variety of fellows for one- to two-year assignments, most of whom had important technical training and experience.[1] As indicated in Figure 4-3, however, the number of fellows has declined significantly in recent years. Of particular concern to the committee responsible for this report has been the sharp reduction in fellows sponsored by the American Association for the Advancement of Science (see Figure 4-4). As of December 2005 there were just five of those fellows in the agency, and the program, at least in its current form, was expected to be terminated this year. The decline in fellows reflects the general constraints on personnel ceilings in the agency and the fact that personnel slots once held by fellows are now being used by staff members who can make a longer-term commitment and can perform such functions as managing contracts that fellows are not authorized to do. In addition, management of the program has been shifted to administrative offices from the technical staffers who had been

---

[1] Including fellows from the following programs: American Association for the Advancement of Science Diplomacy Fellows Program, Johns Hopkins University Health and Child Survival Fellows Program, University of Michigan Population Fellows Program, and Public Health Institute's Population Leadership Program.

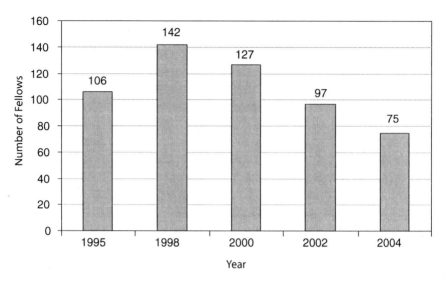

FIGURE 4-3   USAID fellows (1995-2004).

strong advocates for the program. Nonetheless, agency interest in continuing such a program is reflected in plans to issue a request for proposals to operate a new program. One perception of the contribution of AAAS Fellows to USAID programs is set forth in Box 4-1.

BOX 4-1

In the 15 years that USAID has been funding biotechnology programs, these efforts have always been led by former AAAS Fellows. Five former fellows have followed the first one. This continuing influx of new scientific expertise enables USAID to continue to tap new research breakthroughs and to leverage collaborations with the U.S. research community.

SOURCE: Personal communication from a USAID official to committee staff, June 2005.

In addition to efforts to contract for S&T expertise, direct-hire specialists are critical to the effective design and management of projects with S&T content. These projects require good understanding by project managers of technical details. Such understanding is important not only to ensure that the original design of the project is sound but also to assess proposed adjustments during implementation of the projects and to evaluate results and possible next steps. In addition, institution-building projects require insights as to the quality and capabilities of the necessary work force base and the appropriateness of various types of equipment that may be involved. The technical credentials of USAID project managers are critically important in

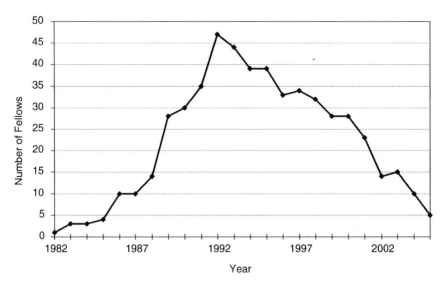

FIGURE 4-4 USAID use of fellows sponsored by the American Association for the Advancement of Science.

gaining respect of partners for the suggestions of the managers. It is simply difficult for USAID officials to manage projects effectively when contractors or other partners have far better understandings of the details of projects than do the USAID managers. Box 4-2 presents an example of how S&T expertise relates to a USAID project.

As agency technical staffs dwindled, the interest within the agency in having specialized "technical" units, particularly in missions, to draw on American S&T resources also declined. Still, S&T have remained integral parts of many agency programs; and retention of a few specialists has been essential. At the same time, the recruitment of new entrants in all disciplines declined until 2001, and each year the S&T age bulge within the staff has moved upward.

USAID's strong economic analysis capability was for many years an important component of its efforts to mobilize S&T in support of development assistance programs. The effectiveness of S&T programs is usually dependent in significant measure on economic policies in the countries where programs are mounted. Unfortunately, the agency's economic analysis capability has declined considerably in recent years.

Similarly, for decades USAID had a strong program evaluation unit, but in recent years that effort has also declined. Such a unit is important for recording both successes and difficulties encountered with innovative projects and for disseminating lessons learned. The USAID Administrator announced in mid-2005 a promising development: a new program to revitalize the evaluation function within the agency.

BOX 4-2
S&T Expertise and Project Development and Implementation

(Activities carried out jointly with appropriate host country institutions)

- Compilation and analysis of technical data that support the need for a project;
- Conceptualization of the project objective and the needed S&T inputs to reach the objective, and identification of the major technical uncertainties and other challenges that will be encountered during implementation;
- Analysis of technical alternatives in designing the project;
- Analysis of project feasibility, including the local capability to use S&T effectively, the availability of financial and human resources to sustain the project over the long term, and the estimated costs to USAID and to the host country;
- Negotiation with the host government and partners of the details of the project, including responses to technical issues that arise;
- Organization of peer review of technical aspects of the project;
- Preparation of persuasive internal USAID documentation supporting the project;
- Monitoring of project implementation and initiating or responding to suggestions for modification of the technical details of the project;
- Evaluation of project results and preparation of documentation on lessons learned; and
- Development of recommendations on next steps.

Given the reduction in size of technical staffs in Washington and the missions, USAID must depend more than ever on its partners—particularly contractors, other U.S. government departments and agencies, and nongovernmental organizations—to provide the technical inputs needed in designing, implementing, and evaluating programs. Fortunately, the staffs of many partners are competent in a variety of technical fields as indicated in Box 4-3. At the same time, the committee received many comments from USAID personnel concerning shortcomings in the technical performance of some contractors. In any event, the agency has become excessively dependent on contractors and other partners as sources of technical expertise.

To be most effective the expertise of partners should be coupled with the

BOX 4-3

USAID contractors have recruited leaders with impressive knowledge of both scientific challenges and local conditions. While there is a rapid turnover of contractors, they have nevertheless quickly found internationally oriented scientists to lead their efforts.

SOURCE: Unpublished report of the NRC Committee on Science and Technology in Foreign Assistance on field visit to Bangladesh, January 2005.

comparable expertise of a strong cadre of direct-hire technical specialists within the agency who participate in internal decisions that determine the strategic directions and program priorities of USAID (see Box 4-4). In addition, well-qualified direct-hire personnel are essential to ensure a credible presence of the agency during interagency and intergovernmental deliberations. Such deliberations often call for stronger support of development of S&T capabilities in developing countries that can help stimulate economic growth and social progress. Contractor personnel are at times torn between their allegiances to their employers and their commitments to respond to approaches of USAID management, which may not be totally consistent with the views of their employers. This apparently was a major concern in developing the program of five-year staff appointments discussed above.

The decline in the number of S&T specialists has significantly reduced advocacy within the agency for exploring opportunities to increase the impact of USAID programs through innovative uses of S&T. Too often technological innovation has become an afterthought that receives little more than lip service in USAID offices, particularly when there are many claimants on limited financial resources. Without technically experienced leaders with direct knowledge of the power and limitations of S&T throughout the agency, the likelihood is low that S&T will obtain a prominent place in discussions of strategies and priorities.

As witnessed during the committee's field visits, there has been an erosion of the capabilities of mission personnel to identify potentially high-payoff opportunities for innovation and to hold their own in technical discussions with well-trained professionals from host countries and other donors. In some cases, technical specialists from other U.S. government agencies are replacing USAID personnel as the interlocutors with important local S&T officials and specialists. Overall, there is a wide variation in the quality of the S&T underpin-

---

BOX 4-4

Mission directors should return to using agency experts to design and manage programs rather than hiring contractors.

SOURCE: USAID Administrator. Report of USAID World Wide Mission Directors Conference, May 17-20, 2005.

BOX 4-5

USAID cannot become a leader in S&T. What the agency can do, however, is coordinate effectively with American scientific agencies in order to ensure that all projects have the optimum access to scientific knowledge. There are many opportunities for USAID to use the scientific and technical capacity of other agencies more effectively.

SOURCE: Unpublished report of the NRC Committee on Science and Technology in Foreign Assistance on field visit to India, November 2004

nings of USAID programs in the field. While a number of USAID's partners have strong S&T competencies, the missions themselves have limited capabilities to effectively mobilize and focus S&T resources. A relevant observation is set forth in Box 4-5.

Finally, the use of peer review within USAID needs prompt attention. While the concept of peer review to enhance the quality of programs and to measure project results is widely accepted within some offices (e.g., US-Israel Research and MERC programs), the approaches used by USAID to determine when and how to carry out peer reviews are sometimes questionable. Often peer reviewers are recruited from existing USAID contractors. In these cases, questions arise as to the independence and objectivity of such arrangements.

STEPS TO ENHANCE S&T CAPABILITIES WITHIN USAID

The committee recommends revitalizing USAID's efforts to harness the power of S&T as an essential input into its programs. Specifically, *USAID should strengthen the capabilities of its leadership and program managers in Washington and in the field to recognize and take advantage of opportunities for effectively integrating S&T considerations within USAID programs.* The following steps would help achieve this objective.

1. *Development of an S&T culture within USAID.* The USAID leadership should continually articulate in policy papers, internal discussions, and interactions with host governments the importance of strengthening local S&T capabilities, integrating these capabilities within a broad range of development activities, and incorporating S&T into USAID programs. The agency should establish training programs and related activities that assist USAID officials engaged in designing, implementing, and evaluating programs to develop a higher degree of science and technology literacy. Within the agency, management should encourage technical specialists to pursue innovative ideas during the program planning processes. This commitment of the USAID leadership to integrate S&T into its programs when appropriate is fundamental in ensuring that suggestions 2 through 7 set forth below can achieve a significant improvement in the agency's use of the nation's S&T resources.

An institutional culture takes years to develop, but the importance of an S&T culture seems obvious as the stakes for developing countries in using S&T effectively are increasing every year. As noted in Chapter 1, those countries—however poor—that successfully integrate modern technologies within their overall approaches to development will have a clear advantage in the rapidly globalizing world. Even the poorest countries can benefit from a limited S&T assessment capability. Therefore, establishment of an S&T culture within USAID that is reflected in field programs should be a long-term agency commitment with near-term as well as long-term payoffs.

The best current example of an institutional culture that permeates USAID is the commitment of employees at all levels in Washington and at all missions to the promotion of good governance. This governance culture has become solidified within USAID as President Bush has made democracy the hallmark of his foreign policy and Congress has dramatically increased appropriations for USAID to support the President's initiative.

Just as good governance provides an important framework for social and economic progress, effective use of S&T should underpin the entire development process.

The Agriculture Strategy adopted by USAID in 2004 is a good example of articulating how S&T can be embedded within the mainstream of USAID programs. This document could serve as a model for setting forth USAID strategies in other fields as well.[2] In addition, employees should be encouraged to think beyond current program approaches and design innovative applications building on the nation's S&T strengths.

With a commitment of the USAID leadership to using American S&T assets more fully, the following suggestions could be very significant.

2. *Strengthening of USAID staff capabilities in S&T.* The professional skills and interests of USAID personnel are a primary determinant of the direction and soundness of agency programs. While the President, Congress, and USAID leadership can mandate priorities and approaches, unless the staff has the wherewithal to carry out directives, the likelihood of successful programs is low. Of course, new initiatives are sometimes coupled with new authorities to hire the required expertise; and these initiatives would seem to have the highest likelihood of success.

Only if there is a new influx of S&T talent will S&T receive adequate attention in USAID programs on a broad scale. Therefore, the agency should recruit assistant administrators, deputy assistant administrators, and mission directors with strong S&T credentials as well as experience in international development for positions that offer special opportunities for improving USAID's use of S&T. Such appointments are particularly important in the pillar bureaus in Washington and in missions in the more technically advanced developing countries. More GS-14 and GS-15 employees with S&T backgrounds are also needed. Bringing S&T expertise directly into the senior levels will significantly increase the sensitivity of the agency to the importance of S&T. Looking to the future, an increased number of entry-level positions should be devoted to young professionals (New Entry Professionals and International Development Interns) with S&T

---

[2]USAID. USAID Agriculture Strategy: Linking Producers to Markets. Washington, DC: USAID, July 2004.

expertise, thereby enhancing the technical capabilities of USAID's Foreign Service (see Appendix L for a description of USAID's recruitment program).

Career incentives for technical specialists to remain at USAID are essential to retaining experience and talent. Promotion opportunities based on an individual's success in applying technical expertise to USAID programs should complement the more common criteria for promotion that are based in large part on the extent of an individual's management responsibilities. Such recognition of the importance of competence and performance in specialized areas of interest to the agency should improve the motivation of skilled S&T specialists to join and remain with USAID.

The continuing efforts of USAID management to increase the overall operating expense budget in order to have funds to cover salaries of an increased number of employees deserve strong support. With an ever-increasing portfolio of programs to manage and while still suffering from staff reductions made during the 1990s, USAID clearly needs personnel enhancements on a broad basis. One of the strongest arguments for overall staff increases is the need to attract and retain technically skilled personnel who are up to date in a variety of S&T areas with high-payoff potential.

Technically trained Foreign Service Nationals (FSNs) work in most USAID missions. They should be given opportunities to stay abreast of S&T developments through participation in relevant training programs and conferences.

3. *Appointment of an S&T Adviser to the Administrator.* During the summer of 2005, the USAID Administrator began to recruit a part-time S&T Adviser. At the end of 2005 the responsibilities and activities of this adviser were still in their formative stages. However, a part-time specialist, even with impressive qualifications, will have little impact on agency policies and programs. While such an adviser might be able to influence some activities in narrow fields, the necessary bureaucratic processes within the agency are simply too formidable for one person to penetrate working part-time.

A full-time S&T Adviser to the Administrator, supported by a small staff, could help ensure that important program opportunities with S&T components are given adequate consideration by the USAID leadership and program managers. A full-time adviser would have time to organize and participate in evaluations of the appropriate use of S&T in USAID's programs and to contribute to particularly important projects. The adviser could help ensure that the agency is well represented in discussions with other departments and agencies, other donors, and host country officials when technical issues are on the table. Of considerable importance, an S&T Adviser could play a central role in guiding the efforts of the Innovation Center and the Advisory Committee discussed later in this chapter (see Figure 4-5).

The S&T Adviser, assisted by a small staff, would have three responsibilities: an **advisory** responsibility for bringing to the attention of the USAID leader-

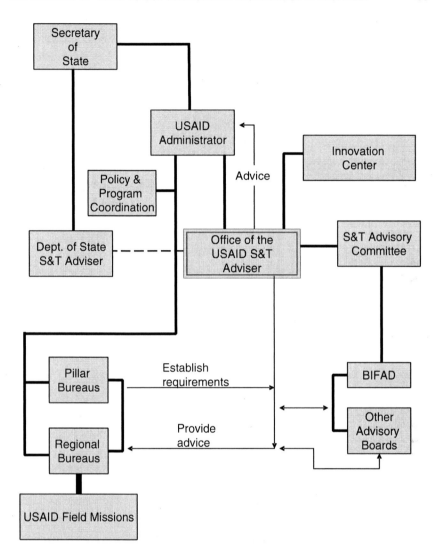

FIGURE 4-5 Strengthening the organizational structure for S&T in USAID.

ship opportunities and issues concerning S&T strategies and specific technologies that are or should be of interest to the agency; a **line** responsibility for overseeing the activities of the Innovation Center; and a **coordination** responsibility for assisting the S&T Advisory Committee in addressing important issues.

The first responsibility would provide insights as to agency priorities and opportunities for the Innovation Center and Advisory Committee to make important contributions. In working with the center and the Advisory Committee, the adviser would be able to compile authoritative assessments for consideration by the agency's leadership. In carrying out all three of these responsibilities, the adviser should give special attention to building an S&T culture throughout the agency, regularly using internal workshops and consultations on specific S&T issues.

The adviser could prepare annual reports for the USAID Administrator on S&T issues before the agency, perhaps in cooperation with the Science and Technology Adviser to the Secretary of State. They could analyze USAID successes and difficulties in incorporating S&T in its programs, but they should not become simply catalogues of S&T projects. The reports could be widely discussed within and outside the agency while they are being prepared. The Administrator could then decide whether the reports should be distributed to senior officials throughout the government and Congress.

Such an adviser will only be successful if positioned appropriately within the agency, perhaps as suggested in Figure 4-5. The adviser needs adequate authority to interact regularly with senior officials throughout the agency. Continuing and prompt access to the administrator is important. An adequate staff is essential so that the adviser can participate effectively in policy determinations and financial resource allocations in a manner that adds value to agency efforts.

In considering the most effective approach to providing a focal point for S&T advice and coordination within the agency, the committee considered three other options that were not as attractive.

1. The committee's interim report suggested that the S&T Adviser to the Secretary of State might have a second responsibility as S&T Adviser to the USAID Administrator. However, the skills and experience required for the two positions are quite different; each position deserves a full-time, high-level specialist, and dual reporting channels would detract from the adviser's effectiveness within USAID.

2. The Science Policy and Environment Office within EGAT could be given an expanded role as the focal point for agency-wide S&T coordination. However, the likelihood is low that an S&T office subsumed in one of the bureaus could be effective across the agency.

3. S&T advisers could be established in each of the three pillar bureaus, but this approach would confuse external partners interested in broad S&T issues and could generate more friction than cooperation within the agency.

4. *Establishment of an S&T Advisory Committee.* A strong but flexible mechanism should be established to provide independent advice on technical issues to the Administrator, assistant administrators, the S&T adviser, program offices, and field missions. Every day, units of the agency are addressing important S&T issues; external advice regarding responses to particularly significant issues could help ensure that complicated developments are well understood. The existing Board on International Food and Agriculture Development (BIFAD) could become a component of the advisory mechanism, although its composition should be carefully reviewed to reduce the possibilities of conflicts of interest.

As to participants in this advisory mechanism, there are many S&T specialists with international development experience who are not dependent on USAID financial support and who would be interested in participating. American universities, research centers of U.S. government departments and agencies, and technology-intensive private firms employ many scientists, engineers, and health professionals who are well respected for independent and objective views.

The Science Advisory Board of the Environmental Protection Agency provides an interesting model that might be adapted to the needs of USAID. A parent board meets several times a year to discuss broad S&T issues. Narrowly focused panels meet more regularly to address specific issues that are of interest to agency leadership or units. The deliberations of the board and panels are captured in technical reports that provide strong supporting documentation in discussions within the Executive Branch as well as between Congress and the Executive Branch.

The committee considered two other approaches to expanding peer review, but they were considered to be less effective. Both approaches have been used in the past by USAID.

1. For more than 20 years the National Academy of Sciences, through a specially constituted Board on Science and Technology in Development, conducted reviews of selected technical issues that were of interest to one or more USAID offices. However, such an external mechanism cannot be tightly linked on a continuing basis to the mainstream of USAID activities—as would be the case with the proposed Advisory Committee. Therefore, it could influence only a narrow range of issues. This was the case with the previous arrangement with the National Academy of Sciences.

2. For decades USAID has convened various types of ad hoc review panels to address emerging technical issues and scientific uncertainties of near-term interest. Too often, however, employees of USAID's financially linked partners have been prominent among the reviewers, largely because they were available and familiar with the specific issues of concern. Other independent reviewers have had difficulty rapidly becoming equally familiar with technical details and only infrequently have had the opportunity for continuing involvement.

5. *Establish a Nongovernmental Innovation Center.* This center, financed by USAID, would concentrate on application of innovative technologies to specific development problems identified by USAID missions, USAID Washington, and the center's staff. A center staff of about 40 technical specialists and 10 managers or administrators, with an annual budget of about $20 million, could give continuing attention to established and emerging technologies and would support mission efforts to help build local technological capacity. Such a staff and budget, while small for a major USAID initiative, should nevertheless be sufficient both to command serious attention within the agency and to support a credible core of specialists who could have a broad impact on agency programs.

The center should differ significantly from sporadic efforts of the past to establish mechanisms for improving capabilities to address innovation issues more effectively. A model for the center could be as follows:

• The center's charter would call for a program of work that emphasizes innovative activities, with the expectation that it would have the resources to field test particularly promising developments in cooperation with USAID missions.

• A senior USAID official with direct links to the USAID Administrator and other senior officials throughout the agency, namely, the S&T Adviser, would serve as the USAID project manager.

• A governing board chaired by USAID's Deputy Administrator and including senior representatives of USAID's regional and pillar bureaus, together with university and industry representatives, would approve the center's program of work within the general framework of the center's charter and evaluate its effectiveness annually.

• There would be an expectation that the center would be sufficiently successful to remain in place for a lengthy period of time (e.g., at least 10 years) thereby providing attractive career enhancement opportunities for the staff.

• The center would have a special responsibility for regularly bringing together USAID's other partners that are working on problems of direct relevance to the center's program of work.

• The center would have both a permanent staff of technical experts and a rotating staff of specialists on assignments from universities, industry, and other appropriate organizations for one to three years (perhaps one-third of the staff) to help ensure that new concepts are considered in the development and implementation of the program of work.

• The center would have a surge capability to respond to particularly important technology-intensive issues of interest to agency offices or missions on a highly selective basis.

The committee considered three other alternatives for increasing the pool of technical specialists who could concentrate on innovative activities, but they were considered less desirable alternatives.

1. **Enhanced in-house capabilities.** It is highly unlikely that direct-hire positions will be allocated to technical specialists to carry out new activities when there is an overriding need for technical personnel to be more involved in management of ongoing programs.

2. **Standard tasking of a selected contractor.** Normal contractual arrange-

ments with other organizations would not provide the necessary clout for the center to be successful nor provide the needed continuity over many years to capitalize on expertise that is developed.

3. **Small groups of narrowly focused S&T specialists within U.S. government agencies.** While selected U.S government agencies would continue their roles as USAID partners, they are not well positioned to take on the broader role envisaged for the center. They would, of course, be important contributors to the center's work.

In proposing the Innovation Center, the committee was well aware that for many years USAID has supported technology innovation projects in a variety of fields that have been carried out by other government agencies, by universities, by nonprofit organizations, and by private companies, usually on an ad hoc basis. However, as discussed throughout this report, innovation activities need sustained reinvigoration in view of the fundamental role of S&T in the development process. The Innovation Center will ensure that a substantial critical mass of effort will be devoted exclusively to the development and introduction of technological innovations into the development process over an extended period. Of course, many shorter-term efforts will continue to be carried out by other organizations supported by USAID, underscoring the importance of coordination across the agency and with other assistance providers.

The committee is not aware of any organization that has characteristics similar to those of the proposed Innovation Center. However, in designing the center, USAID should examine the experience of other organizations that have been involved in selected aspects of innovation and development; for example, experiences of the Battelle Memorial Institute (industrial technologies, medical technologies), the National Renewable Energy Laboratory, and Enterprise Works/VITA (small-scale technologies) should be helpful in developing approaches for the Innovation Center.

6. Strengthening the economic analysis capability of USAID. Economic policies have a profound influence on prospects for sustainable economic development, including development dependent on the use of effective and affordable technologies. USAID leaders recognize that the steady decline of economics capability within USAID needs to be reversed (see Box 4-6). This is certainly

BOX 4-6
Expand recruitment of economists and engineers.
SOURCE: Agreed follow-up at USAID Worldwide Mission Directors Conference, May 2005.

true if program managers are to (1) understand and promote fundamental policy reforms that support development and growth, (2) encourage the creation of business-friendly environments for private sector firms in host countries, and

(3) recognize the many dimensions of technological change occurring in almost every developing country. Of particular importance, support by USAID of the introduction and development of specific technologies requires careful assessments of the long-term financial implications of proposed projects.

In some cases USAID can rely on the work of the World Bank and other organizations that have strong economic analysis units and recognize the importance of the private sector contribution to development. But it is essential for USAID to have a strong economics staff since understanding and promoting appropriate economic policies, at both the macro and the micro level, is critical to USAID's development mission.

The one-person professional staff in EGAT responsible for micro-economic reform projects has commendable ambitions but cannot respond to many of the requests for assistance. The principal activity of the unit is to arrange for economic specialists to go to the missions and provide advice on specific issues, activities that often reflect requests from host governments for short-term economics expertise related to promoting private sector investment.

7. *Revitalizing the program evaluation capability of the agency.* USAID's once-robust capability to carry out rigorous evaluations of program effectiveness has declined, making it difficult for USAID to understand the reasons for the success or failure of particular programs. Restoration of this capability is important in providing lessons learned from all types of projects, including those that have involved S&T. Projects focused on S&T must overcome many hurdles, and past successes can provide useful pointers for the future. The successes in using remote-sensing technologies and biotechnology are but two examples of lessons learned that should be easily retrievable.

USAID contractors can carry out some evaluation activities, of course. But well-qualified direct-hire professionals are needed to guide the design of evaluation methodologies, to coordinate within USAID feasible approaches to carry out evaluations that should involve the missions, and to bring to the attention of agency managers lessons learned from USAID projects. In addition, a career staff is essential to ensure that the initial momentum in ramping up the program is maintained and to draw continually on lessons learned in years past as new initiatives are considered by program offices.

In summary, a number of steps have been suggested above to enable USAID to use S&T more effectively in its programs. They should be an important point of departure for upgrading the agency's S&T capabilities.

On several occasions during the course of the study, USAID officials asked the committee to provide estimates of the number of new S&T-related positions that are required to provide the agency with an internal capability such as that set forth above to take full advantage of U.S. S&T assets. During these discussions, a senior USAID official estimated for the committee that the number of additional direct-hire scientists and engineers, both civil service and foreign service that are needed within USAID is in the range of 50 to 150. The committee has no basis for disputing the estimate. A detailed work force analysis by specialists familiar with USAID's entire portfolio and sensitive to the importance of S&T skills during the age of globalization is required to arrive at a well-considered number. Nevertheless, in order to be responsive to the USAID request, a very preliminary estimate of the personnel requirements to implement the recommendation in this chapter is offered by the committee, keeping in mind the estimate of 50 to 150 positions:

- At least 10 of the approximately 100 assistant administrators, deputy assistant administrators, and mission directors should have strong S&T backgrounds.
- Fifteen new direct-hire positions at the GS-14 or GS-15 levels for specialists with strong S&T backgrounds are needed.
- Five direct-hire positions are needed in the Office of the S&T Adviser.
- Five new direct-hire positions are needed in the economics unit of EGAT.
- Three new direct-hire positions are need in the program evaluation unit.
- The intake of AAAS Fellows should increase to 15-20 each year.
- Recruitment of 15-20 New Entry Professionals with strong S&T background should be carried out each year.

For too long USAID has been forced to substitute personnel from contractors and other government agencies for needed direct-hire employees with strong S&T capabilities and has lagged behind in identifying and using opportunities for technological innovation in a number of fields. The initiatives proposed in this chapter will be important steps in restoring the expertise needed to draw effectively on the nation's powerful S&T assets in foreign assistance.

5

USAID'S Coordination with Other U.S. Government Departments and Agencies

Capitalizing on USAID's Unique Field Perspective

This chapter addresses coordination among U.S. government departments and agencies in Washington and overseas locations as they deal with S&T-related issues that are within the broad legislative mandate of USAID. The emphasis is on actions that USAID can take to improve coordination, recognizing that the Department of State often has the lead in ensuring appropriate coordination.

The chapter does not address coordination of USAID programs with those of other donors, international organizations, NGOs, multinational companies, or other organizations interested in foreign assistance. Such broader coordination is an important and complicated issue that is particularly significant in helping to ensure wise use of limited international resources. However, the topic of coordination with all parties interested in foreign assistance is beyond the scope of this study.

About 40 U.S. government departments and agencies have bilateral and regional programs involving developing countries. S&T are prominent themes in many of these programs. The programs are, in the first instance, designed to contribute to achievement of the missions of the departments and agencies, missions that have become increasingly international as globalization becomes a more prominent aspect of government-wide policies and programs. Some programs in developing countries contribute to economic and social development of the cooperating developing countries as well; but this aspect is usually an objective of secondary importance to U.S. departments and agencies as they extend their global reaches.

Several examples of the expanding interests of U.S. departments and agencies underscore the breadth of U.S. government activities abroad. At the top of the list, the Department of State is vitally concerned as to the impacts of foreign assistance in all target countries. The social and economic development of these countries directly affects many U.S. foreign policy objectives, including (1) promoting global and regional stability, (2) supporting U.S. private sector investments abroad, (3) ensuring U.S. access to important energy and other natural resources, and (4) countering the spread of terrorist groups. The Department of State has increasingly taken on management responsibilities for operational programs in the developing countries, and particularly the President's Emergency Program for AIDS Relief (PEPFAR). The Department of State plays a lead role in determining the purposes and levels of U.S. contributions to international organizations that have many programs in developing countries.

Of special relevance to this study are the interests of the Department of State's Office of Oceans and International Environmental and Scientific Affairs (OES). The office is, of course, interested in USAID's activities that provide new channels for international cooperation and communication but has not shown comparable interest in the development of S&T capacity in developing countries. OES has limited program funds that it has used on occasion for environmental and other activities in the developing countries. The office has for many years developed strategic plans for addressing S&T-related issues throughout the world, and these plans inevitably overlap with the interests of USAID when addressing developing countries.[1] The level of coordination among OES, the department's science and environmental officers in U.S. embassies in developing countries, and USAID program officers is inconsistent, and depends largely on the breadth of experience and interests of the officials involved. Of course, communication among all parties on issues of mutual concern should be strongly encouraged, but attempts to strengthen coordination of USAID's program interests with the interests of OES through new bureaucratic requirements should be undertaken with great care lest such efforts complicate rather than improve the effectiveness of USAID's programs and OES's policies.

We saw a highly visible example of interagency coordination reflected in Figure 1-1: the many streams of U.S. financing of programs to combat HIV/AIDS worldwide, including indirect financing through international organizations. The PEPFAR program, in particular, has provided considerable stimulus for improved coordination of U.S. activities abroad. U.S. ambassadors are explicitly charged by the administration to personally lead the coordination. In some countries the ambassadors have extended this coordination to encompass all U.S.-financed health programs.

---

[1] See, for example, NRC. Goals, strategies, and objectives in the program plan of the Bureau of Oceans and International Environmental and Scientific Affairs. *In* The Pervasive Role of Science, Technology, and Health in Foreign Policy, Imperatives for the Department of State, pp. 106-111. Washington, D.C.: National Academy Press, 1999.

TABLE 5-1 The National Institute of Allergy and Infectious Diseases' Research Activities on HIV/AIDS, TB, and Malaria in Sub-Saharan Africa

NIAID supports projects in 25 countries. Examples include:

- **Adult AIDS Clinical Trials Group**—a net work on clinical sites that investigates therapeutic interventions for HIV/AIDS infection and its complications in adults.
- **International Collaborations in Infectious Disease Research**—to promote interaction between U.S. investigators and scientists in a host country where tropical diseases are endemic.
- **Tuberculosis Research Unite**—translates advances in TB research into new tools for improved clinical trials.
- **Pediatric AIDS Clinical Trails Group**—network of clinical sites that evaluates clinical interventions for treating HIV/AIDS infection and its complications in neonates, infants, children, adolescents, and pregnant women.

SOURCE: NIAID. Communication with Committee, March 2005.

The Department of Defense and the Department of State undertake major efforts in facilitating the transition from U.S. military occupation of war-torn areas to stable civilian governments. The Department of Defense is also actively involved in strengthening the technological capabilities of developing nations, which assists in resisting military invasions and strengthening the base for civilian activities. The Department of Health and Human Services has extensive programs to contain infectious diseases and combat other health problems on every continent. Table 5-1 describes the extensive efforts of the National Institute of Allergy and Infectious Diseases in southern Africa. The National Science Foundation supports scientific cooperation of researchers from many developing countries to address issues of considerable importance to American scientists and engineers as well as being of interest in their own countries. The Centers for Disease Control and Prevention, U.S. Department of Agriculture, Environmental Protection Agency, National Oceanic and Atmospheric Administration, and National Aeronautics and Space Administration also have active programs that span the globe.

For decades USAID has provided funding to various U.S. government departments and agencies to manage implementation of USAID programs that have technical content of direct interest to the departments and agencies. For example, the Department of Agriculture and the Centers for Disease Control and Prevention manage USAID projects in dozens of countries. Usually the projects are fully or largely funded by USAID, but on occasion there is cost sharing between USAID and the implementing organization. These other organizations often have their own programs in developing countries—funded directly through congressional appropriations—that are relevant to USAID's interests.

The establishment of the Millennium Challenge Corporation (MCC) in 2003 has added a new dimension to foreign assistance. With an annual budget in the billions of dollars, this independent organization provides financing in response to requests from governments of developing countries (23 developing countries as of late 2005) that are on sound paths to "ruling justly, investing in people, and encouraging economic freedom." The MCC has had a slow startup; but the availability of substantial funding after programs are launched seems secure, even though the level is not as high as anticipated in 2003 (because of the initial delays).

As discussed in Chapter 2, another area of interagency significance is providing early warning of and response to natural disasters. In this area USAID depends on support from other departments and agencies. In particular, the Department of Defense has many types of capabilities that are often deployed when there are such emergencies. Sometimes they are deployed at the request of USAID and are financed by USAID. On other occasions they are deployed at the initiative of the White House, the Department of State, or the Department of Defense itself, and in these instances the funding responsibility is less certain and determined case by case. In any event, with many departments and agencies involved—let alone other governments, international organizations, and NGOs—coordination is critical; and USAID is usually the coordination point for the U.S. government.

Technologies play important roles in such responses and in coordination of responses. Communications technologies linking the international responses to the activities of the affected governments are particularly critical. Appropriate international sharing of responsibilities for different types of activities—from providing food supplements to arranging for evacuation of damaged areas—is essential, and computer databases loom large in promoting and monitoring such sharing. Damage assessments through use of satellite and aerial photography in coordination with on-the-ground observations are also a high priority. Governments and NGOs often send teams of scientists to the scene to record observations that will be helpful in predicting future disasters and improving response strategies; sharing of information is important for the success of such missions.

According to the USAID Administrator, USAID now funds only about 50 percent of U.S. government foreign assistance. Thus, the intersection of USAID programs and the interests of other departments and agencies are manifold. As discussed throughout this report, S&T inevitably permeate many of these programs. The importance of effective coordination of the multiplicity of programs is clear and must be a high-priority responsibility of department and agency leaders in Washington and U.S. ambassadors around the world.

USAID has unique legislative authority of great breadth to support innovative programs in developing countries, unrivaled field experience in adapting technological advances to conditions and capabilities of poor countries, and many successes in integrating S&T into development activities. Therefore, the agency should continue to play a critical role in S&T-related programs of the U.S. government throughout the developing world.

To this end, the committee recommends that ***USAID encourage other U.S. departments and agencies with S&T-related activities in developing countries*** *to orient their programs to the extent possible to supporting the development priorities of the host countries; USAID should provide leadership in improving coordination of U.S.-government.-sponsored activities relevant to development.*

As previously noted, both in Washington and overseas the need for interagency approaches that are mutually reinforcing and for coordination of overlapping activities is increasing. As repeatedly emphasized in this report, USAID's field perspectives should be effectively integrated with the strong S&T assessment and programming capabilities of a number of other organizations. Therefore, USAID should:

1. *Assume leadership in the establishment in Washington of an effective interagency committee to coordinate overlapping S&T interests of U.S. departments and agencies in developing countries.* USAID, in cooperation with the Office of Science and Technology Policy and the Department of State, should take a leading role in bringing together the departments and agencies. USAID should ensure that such an arrangement does not deteriorate just into sessions wherein other agencies request funds from USAID. Rather, the agency needs to emphasize the importance of coordination on topics that have significant development potential, whatever the funding source. These topics include:

1. The development and implementation of bilateral S&T agreements promoted by the Department of State, which in the past has too often turned to USAID for financial support of already agreed programs that are of little interest to USAID;

2. USDA programming of PL-480 funds that directly overlap USAID interests (see Box 5-1);

3. NASA remote-sensing programs that could add new dimensions to USAID agricultural and environmental efforts;

4. CDC disease surveillance activities that should complement USAID health programs; and

---

BOX 5-1

The Department of Agriculture is developing a program to provide grants for agricultural research through the Bangladesh Academy of Sciences using PL-480 funds available to the U.S. government. The USAID mission knows nothing about this academy nor was the mission consulted on the design of the program even though the mission has a major interest in agricultural research.

SOURCE: Unpublished report of the NRC Committee on Science and Technology in Foreign Assistance on field visit to Bangladesh, January 2005.

5. Department of Commerce's capacity-building programs for international trade that are related to USAID's efforts to promote economic growth.

The interagency committee should focus its attention both on policy coordination in Washington and on coordination of on-the-ground activities in the field. The interagency committee could review annually the drafts of the country strategies prepared by U.S. embassies in five or six countries where USAID has major programs. The committee could then provide feedback to the embassies concerning opportunities for increasing the impacts by more fully integrating the program interests of different departments and agencies.

There is, of course, a variety of coordination mechanisms already in place in Washington. Although the former interagency committee on international activities[2] established in the 1990s by the Office of Science and Technology Policy no longer exists, the National Technology Council, a White House coordinating council, has taken on several international topics. At present the Department of State brings together representatives of a large number of departments and agencies to address a variety of S&T-related issues that have development relevance, such as (1) global climate change, (2) AIDS/HIV programs, and (3) S&T in the former Soviet Union. USAID regularly convenes interagency meetings to deal with disasters and other humanitarian emergencies. There is, however, no mechanism to address S&T-related development challenges on a broad and continuing basis. The proposed interagency committee should not duplicate the many efforts underway but should be aware of them in its deliberations.

2. Emphasize within the joint State Department-USAID planning process and in the field the payoff from broad interagency coordination of S&T activities. The administrator and mission directors of USAID should continually advise the U.S. ambassadors at posts where USAID is active of the important contributions that USAID can make in developing U.S. country strategies that encompass S&T. The mission directors should be strong advocates for broad coordination in their daily activities.

3. Clarify the division of responsibilities for supporting research relevant to international development supported by USAID and by other U.S. government departments and agencies. In general, USAID should concentrate its resources on identifying opportunities to use scientific achievements in the field, and facilitating their adaptation and introduction, leaving other aspects of research to others. Delineations that are more precise should be sector specific and at times project specific. Table 5-2 presents a suggested role for USAID in the

---

[2]Committee on International Science, Engineering, and Technology (CISET).

TABLE 5-2 Improving Health Outcomes: Role of USAID in the New Global Landscape for Research on Special Problems of Developing Countries.

	Health Assessment/ Priority Setting	Basic Research	Applied Research/Development/ Adaptation	Field Implementation and Evaluation
Task	Disease surveillance Assessments of burden of disease Identification of Critical Knowledge Gaps		Product development Field trials Consumer research Modification of existing products	Adaptation at scale Strengthening national health systems Monitor program effectiveness and modify approaches
Performance	Local agencies USAID (major)/ CDC Bilateral donors	NIH Pharmaceutical companies International foundations Local research organizations	Pharmaceutical and medical supply companies Local research organizations USAID Bilateral donors	Local agencies USAID (major) Global fund WHO Bilateral donors PEPFAR

Improved Health Outcomes

health sector. In the agriculture sector the environmental uniqueness of different locations suggests that USAID needs to reach further back in supporting research. In the energy field, applications may be more appropriately left to the private sector.

4. *Work with other government organizations involved in preventing and responding to natural disasters in order to strengthen the capacity of developing countries* to improve early warning systems, upgrade the resilience of physical structures to impacts, increase availability of emergency social support resources, and develop response strategies that can be integrated with long-term development programs.

An important starting point is to ensure that internal mechanisms are in place within USAID for handing off responsibilities for combating disasters over the long-term from the disaster response offices that are concerned with immediate problems to development assistance offices that are responsible for the long term, and then to draw on the capabilities of other agencies to upgrade warning and response capabilities in the developing countries.

5. *Work closely with the Departments of State and Defense and other national and international organizations involved in reconstruction of war-torn areas,* taking advantage of the technical capabilities of these partners while sharing USAID's experience in charting the course for recovery. Current experience in Iraq, Afghanistan, and Kosovo underscores how important it is for USAID to have strong engineering capabilities within the agency and its partners to provide near-term relief for decimated populations.

6. *Develop programs that complement the programs of the Department of State* for combating HIV/AIDS, tuberculosis, and malaria. USAID, among the many organizations interested in combating HIV/AIDS, should capitalize on its unique field capabilities to build local capabilities for delivering health services. As suggested in Table 5-2, USAID's emphasis should be on assessing the public health situation and on implementing and evaluating the impacts of field programs.

7. *Encourage the Millennium Challenge Corporation (MCC) to take advantage of USAID's many years of experience in promoting international development in the countries where the MCC has decided to initiate programs.* The USAID Administrator, as a member of the MCC board, should ensure that the board and staff involve USAID specialists in consultations with recipient governments and in reviews of proposals by these governments. The early praise set forth in Box 5-2 suggests that USAID is indeed contributing to the initial activities of the MCC.

The pooling of expertise and financial resources has enabled USAID to have impacts far beyond those that its own capabilities would allow. The importance

---

BOX 5-2

We could not have done our job in our first startup year without you, the USAID mission directors. We want to preserve and expand USAID funding; you do things we cannot do that are essential to the fight against poverty . . . MCC is allocating $180 million to USAID to help several threshold countries become eligible for assistance and in all cases MCC teams will depend on USAID teams to provide knowledge of the countries and local officials.

SOURCE: Statement of the President of MCC at the USAID Worldwide Mission Directors Conference, May 17-20, 2005.

---

of such coordination is increasing, and steps are urgently required to ensure that expanding programs enhance and not detract from USAID's mission.

Implementation of the foregoing suggestions will require considerable USAID staff time. The USAID staff enhancements suggested in Chapter 4 would contribute directly to the improvement of interagency coordination. Even without additional staff, limited upgrading of coordination should be possible.

Epilogue

S&T are integral components of most development activities. The better the S&T base for these activities, the greater the likelihood for social and economic progress in the developing countries. Judging from the field visits of the committee and from discussions by committee members with a large number of foreign assistance practitioners, many developing country governments realize that long-term progress depends in significant measure on their ability to use S&T effectively.

This report sets forth a number of recommendations and suggestions for enhancing the capabilities of USAID to contribute to building appropriate S&T capacity in the countries where it has programs. It highlights the overriding importance of increasing the S&T capabilities of USAID's foreign service and civil service employees. It emphasizes that while its partners provide important S&T capabilities, strengthened internal staffs are essential to guide the programs of the agency that rely on S&T expertise.

All of the recommendations set forth in this report could be implemented at the direction of the USAID Administrator and his senior staff, with the exception of the recommendation to establish an S&T advisory committee which would require approval by the Office of Management and Budget. But it will not be an easy task to convince the USAID leadership to embrace S&T more fully when there are so many competing demands for personnel slots and financial resources. To this end, this report can provide a basis for follow-up discussions by the S&T proponents, within and outside USAID, with the Agency and Congressional leaderships.

If there are decisions within USAID to move forward in the S&T arena on a significant scale, the implementation of programs that are developed will require tenacity and determination by the S&T proponents over a period of years. Indeed, sustaining the effort for the indefinite future should there be a decline in the foreign assistance budget will be a difficult task. But the development payoff from better access to S&T achievements by populations of developing countries and the rewards for the security of the United States from new international partnerships in critical technological areas are potentially very great. Therefore, even though the outcome a decade into the future from this proposed S&T initiative cannot be predicted with certainty, the stakes are so great that a decision by the USAID Administrator to provide significant resources for S&T-related activities at this time is fully warranted.

APPENDIXES

Appendix A

Statement of Task from Cooperative Agreement

A Committee of the National Research Council (NRC) will assess new opportunities for the U.S. Agency for International Development (USAID) and its partners to draw on the science, engineering, and medical resources of the nation in designing and carrying out foreign assistance programs. The assessment will recommend steps that USAID should consider in enhancing its capabilities to use these resources for addressing the challenges of international development in the years ahead. Among the recent developments of interest to USAID that will be considered are (a) the expanding science and technology interests of the Department of State and their relationship to the activities of USAID, (b) the role of the Millennium Challenge Account (MCA), and (c) the establishment of partnerships that link USAID with international, regional, U.S. governmental, and private sector foundations and other organizations.

This project will examine selected aspects of USAID's activities that have benefited or could benefit from access to strong science, technology, and medical capabilities. The activities to be considered, while only a portion of the large number of relevant programs and projects, will span the full range of development assistance, humanitarian assistance, and economic support. Of special importance are programs in fields such as health care, agriculture and nutrition, energy, and the environment. Cutting across these sectors are programs directed to education and job creation as well as the strengthening of enabling technologies in areas such as information and communications.

Appendix B

Biographies of Committee Members

Thomas Pickering (co-chair) is senior vice president for international relations of the Boeing Company. He assumed this position in 2001 and oversees the company's international affairs, including those involving foreign governments. Ambassador Pickering served as Under Secretary of State for Political Affairs from 1997 to 2000. Prior to that, he briefly held the position of president of the Eurasia Foundation. In a diplomatic career spanning five decades he served as U.S. ambassador to the Russian Federation, India, Israel, El Salvador, Nigeria, and Jordan. From 1989 to 1992 he was the U.S. representative to the United Nations.

Kenneth Shine (co-chair) (IOM) is vice chancellor for health affairs of the University of Texas System. Previously he was the director of the Center for Domestic and International Health Security at the RAND Corporation. He was the president of the Institute of Medicine from 1992 to 2002. He is a professor of medicine emeritus at the School of Medicine, University of California, Los Angeles, where he has also served as dean and provost for Medical Sciences.

Barry Bloom (NAS/IOM) is dean of the faculty of the School of Public Health and professor of immunology and infectious diseases at Harvard University. He has been extensively involved with the World Health Organization for more than 30 years. Dr. Bloom served on the U.S. AIDS Vaccine Research Committee and the National Advisory Board of the Fogarty International Center. He chairs the Board of Trustees for the International Vaccine Institute in South Korea. He also has served on the National Advisory Council of the National Institute of Allergy and Infectious Diseases, the Scientific Advisory Board of the National Center for Infectious Diseases, and the Governing Board of the Institute of Medicine.

Owen Cylke manages a collaborative project with the World Bank on issues of trade liberalization, rural poverty, and the environment within the World Wildlife Fund's Macroeconomics for Sustainable Development Program. From 1993 to 2002 Mr. Cylke was director of the Policy Group, a development initiative of Winrock International and the Tata Energy and Resources Institute supported by the U.S.-Asia Environmental Partnership. Earlier Mr. Cylke served as president of the Association of Big Eight Universities (1989-1992). At USAID from 1966 to 1989, he was deputy assistant administrator for Food and Voluntary Assistance, director of the Economic Assistance Mission to India, and deputy director of the Economic Assistance Missions to Egypt and Afghanistan.

Lee Hamilton has been the director of the Woodrow Wilson International Center for Scholars since 1999. Previously he served for 34 years as a U.S. congressman from Indiana. He was a leading congressional voice on foreign affairs, with particular interests in promoting democracy and market reform in the former Soviet Union and Eastern Europe, promoting peace and stability in the Middle East, expanding U.S. markets and trade overseas, and overhauling U.S. export and foreign aid policies. Mr. Hamilton has also been a leading national figure on economic policy and congressional organization.

Susanna Hecht is a professor of urban planning and the associate director of the University of California, Los Angeles, Latin American Center. Her research interests include the political economy of tropical rain forest development, women in development, international environmental politics, and environmental history. Her current research analyzes the dynamics of decentralization and democratization on patterns of deforestation in the Brazilian and Bolivian Amazon. She is also involved in a project in Central America and Mexico that uses remote sensing and ethnography.

Susan Henry is the dean of the College of Agriculture and Life Sciences and professor of molecular biology and genetics at Cornell University. From 1991 to 2000 she was the dean of the Carnegie Mellon College of Science. She is a member of the Committee on Election to Fellowship and of the Board of Governors Nominating Committee, American Academy of Microbiology. She is the past chair of the National Institutes of Health Advisory Committee on Research on Minority Health. Dr. Henry's research is supported by NIH.

David Hopper has an extensive career in the field of sustainable development and economic and agricultural policy. From 1978 to 1987 he was vice president for the South Asia region at the World Bank. He retired from the World Bank in

1990 after three years as a senior vice president for Policy, Planning, and Research. In 1970 he became the first president of the International Development Research Centre in Canada. Prior to that time he was a professor until 1962, when he joined the Ford Foundation and then the Rockefeller Foundation as an agricultural economist in India. Since retiring from the World Bank, he has taken senior positions at Haldor Topsoe Inc., Ontario Hydro International Inc., D&R Associates International, and Acres International Inc.

Michael T. Rock is a professor and chair of the Department of Economics of Bryn Mawr College. He previously served as professor and chair of the Department of Economics at Hood College. From 1994 to 1999 he worked as a senior economist at Winrock International Institute for Agricultural Development, after serving as a professor of economics at the Institute of International Relations, Hanoi, Vietnam. He worked at the U.S. Agency for International Development as director of the AID Staff Strengthening through Environmental Training (ASSET) Program from 1992 to 1993. From 1986 to 1992 he was director of USAID's Development Studies Program.

Allan Rosenfield (IOM) has been dean of the School of Public Health at Columbia University since 1986. He is also professor of Obstetrics-Gynecology and Public Health. In 1966, he finished his medical training and subsequently spent one year as an instructor in the Department of Obstetrics and Gynecology at the University of Lagos Teaching Hospital in Nigeria and six years as Medical Advisor to the Ministry of Public Health in Thailand. Dr. Rosenfield has served as president of the New York Obstetrical Society, chair of the Executive Board of the American Public Health Association, and chair of the boards of the Planned Parenthood Federation of America, AVSC International, and the Alan Guttmacher Institute. He is currently chairman of the New York State Department of Health AIDS Advisory Council, and president-elect of the Association of Schools of Public Health.

Philip M. Smith is a science organization executive and policy consultant. From 1981 to mid-1994, he was executive officer of the National Academy of Sciences and National Research Council. For more than 20 years he was a government research management and science and technology policy official with the White House Office of Science and Technology Policy, Office of Management and Budget, and National Science Foundation.

Barry Worthington has been the executive director of the United States Energy Association since 1988, responsible for the Association's domestic and international activities. Previously he served as a vice president of the Thomas Alva Edison Foundation. Mr. Worthington also serves as chairman of the National Energy Foundation and is a member of the Board of Directors of the World

Environment Center and the U.S.-China Energy Environment Center, as well as trustee of the Energy & Mineral Law Foundation. He has written extensively on energy and environmental matters, and addresses many conferences on national and international energy issues

Appendix C

Field Visits and
Key Organizations Contacted

India Field Visit (Health), August 14-21, 2004

Panel members

Kenneth Shine, committee co-chair, University of Texas System, Office of
    Health Affairs
Helen Smits, committee consultant, IOM member, former deputy administrator
    of the Health Care Financing Administration
Rosalyn Hobson, USAID liaison, Virginia Commonwealth University
Pat Koshel, staff member, National Research Council

Key organizations contacted

U.S. Embassy
USAID Mission
World Health Organization
Department of Biotechnology
Department of Health and Family Welfare
Indian Council of Medical Research
Commercial Market Strategies (CMS)
PATH-India (Program for Appropriate Technologies in Health)
Project Avahan (India AIDS Initiative)
Bill and Melinda Gates Foundation
CORE Group Polio Project
Environmental Health Project (EHP)

IndiaCLEN (Indian Clinical Epidemiology Network)
Gurgaon District Tuberculosis Center
Department of Cardiology, All India Institute of Medical Sciences

Philippines Field Visit (Energy), November 7-11, 2004

Panel members

Barry Worthington, committee member, United States Energy Association
Philip Smith, committee member, consultant
Rosalyn Hobson, USAID liaison, Virginia Commonwealth University
Christopher Holt, staff member, National Research Council

Key organizations contacted

U.S. Embassy
USAID Mission
• Office of Population and Nutrition
• Office of Energy and Environment
Philippines Department of Energy
U.S. Department of Energy, Sustainable Energy Development Program
Asian Development Bank
Infinite Progression Corporation
Mirant Philippines Foundation, Inc.
PA Consulting
Petron Corporation
Philippine National Oil Company
Shell Philippines and Shell Renewable
University of the Philippines, Department of Engineering
Winrock International, Alliance for Mindanao Off-grid Renewable Energy
    Program (AMORE)

Guatemala and El Salvador Field Visit (Biological Diversity Conservation), January 10-14, 2005

Panel members

Michael Clegg, ex-officio committee member, University of California, Irvine,
    foreign secretary of the National Academy of Sciences
Anthony Stocks, committee consultant, Idaho State University
Sara Gray, staff member, National Research Council

Key organizations contacted

USAID/Guatemala, Central American Program Office
Centro Agronómico Tropical de Investigación y Enseñanza
Ministerio de Ambiente y Recursos Naturales
The Nature Conservancy
Consejo Nacional de Areas Protegidas
Fortalecimiento Institutional en Politicas Ambientales
Biofor project
Programa Salvadoreño Investigación Sobre Desarrollo y Medio Ambiente
CCAD (Central American Commission for Environment and Development)
Biofor Project, Petén
Wildlife Conservation Society
Asociación de Comunidades Forestales de Petén

Bangladesh Field Visit (Agriculture and Food Security), January 14-22, 2005

Panel members

Susan Henry, committee member, Cornell University
Charles Hess, committee consultant, University of California, Davis
Rosalyn Hobson, USAID liaison, Virginia Commonwealth University
Glenn Schweitzer, project director, National Research Council

Key organizations contacted

U.S. Embassy
USAID Mission
ATDP II (Agro-based Industries and Technology Development Project)
World Fish
Winrock International
CARE Bangladesh
International Centre for Diarrheal Disease Research, BD (ICDDR,B)
International Maize and Wheat Improvement Center (CIMMYT)
Bangladesh Agricultural Research Council (BARC)
Bangladesh Agricultural Research Institute (BARI)
Bangladesh Rice Research Institute (BRRI)
Wheat Research Center (WRC)
Horticulture Research Center (HRC)
The World Bank Resident Mission
Food and Agriculture Organization (FAO)
Asian Development Bank

Mali Field Visit (Poverty in a resource deficient country), February 26-March 6, 2005

Panel members

Owen Cylke, committee member, World Wildlife Fund
John Lewis, committee consultant, ProNatura USA
Rosalyn Hobson, USAID liaison, Virginia Commonwealth University
Laura Holliday, staff member, National Research Council

Key organizations contacted

U.S. Embassy
USAID Mission
OECD Paris, Sahel West Africa Club
Office of Food Security, Office of the President
Ministry of Education
  • National Center for Scientific and Technical Research
Ministry of Environment
Ministry of Agriculture/CNRA
  • Central Veterinary Laboratory (CVL)
European Union Coordination Office
Agence Française de Développement
Netherlands Embassy
World Bank Office
Coordinator CSLP (Poverty Reduction Strategy)
Cinzana Research Station (Institut d'Economie Rurale [IER])
Primature (MCC)
Institut d'Economie Rurale (IER)
International Crops Research Institute for the Semi-Arid Tropics (ICRISAT)
Syngenta Foundation
University of Mali
  • Engineering School
Biotech Laboratory
Compagnie Malienne pour le Dévelopement des Textiles (CMDT [Malian Company for Textile Development])
PRODEPAM, Mali Finance, Trade Mali (USAID/AEG contractors)
Malaria Research Laboratory and HIV Laboratory (supported by NIH)
Michigan State University Office
Institut du Sahel
Soils CRSP Office
Club du Sahel, Agricultural Transformation and Sustainable Development

Appendix D

USAID Offices Consulted in Washington

Office of the Administrator
- Administrator
- Global Development Alliance Secretariat

Bureau for Latin America and the Caribbean
- Central America and Mexico Regional Strategy Office
- Office of Environment

Bureau for Africa
- Office of West African Affairs

Bureau for Policy Development and Program Coordination

Bureau for Management
- Office of Human Resources
- Office of Information Resources Management

Bureau for Democracy, Conflict, and Assistance
- Office of Food for Peace
- Office of Transition Initiatives

Office of American Schools and Hospitals Abroad
- Office of Human Capacity Development

Bureau of Global Health
- Office of Health, Infectious Diseases, and Nutrition

Bureau for Economic Growth, Agriculture, and Trade
- Office of Agriculture
- Office of Energy and Information Technology
- Office of Natural Resources Management
- Office of Environment and Science Policy

Appendix E

Other Organizations Consulted

Office of Science and Technology Policy

Office of Management and Budget

Department of State
- Bureau for Oceans, Environment, and International Scientific Affairs
- Office of the Science and Technology Adviser to the Secretary

Centers for Disease Control and Prevention

National Institutes of Health
- Office of the Director
- National Institute of Allergy and Infectious Diseases
- Fogarty International Center

Environmental Protection Agency

Millennium Challenge Corporation

The World Bank
- Environmentally and Socially Sustainable Development Program
- Office of the Coordinator of Scientific and Technological Affairs

United Nations
- Executive Office of the Secretary General
- United Nations Development Program

Conservation International
- Center for Applied Biodiversity Science

Association Liaison Office for University Cooperation in Development

PATH (Program for Appropriate Technology for Health)

Partnership to End Hunger in Africa

The Nature Conservancy

World Wildlife Fund

RAND Corporation

Bill & Melinda Gates Foundation
- Global Health Program

United States Energy Association, Energy Partnership Program

International Foundation for Science

Appendix F

Report to Congress:
Health-Related Research and Development Activities at USAID

June 2005

EXECUTIVE SUMMARY

Congress requested that the U.S. Agency for International Development (USAID) provide a report describing its role in the research, development, and application cycle and its efforts to coordinate research and development activities with other agencies. This report responds to this request and provides details on the amounts spent on research by health issue or disease, recipient, and stage of research or development funded.

From 2002 to 2004, USAID invested between 6 and 7 percent of its total health-related budget in research and development. In 2004, this percentage represented $155 million. That year, the largest amount of research funds was spent on HIV/AIDS related research, followed in descending order by research on family planning and reproductive health, research on infectious diseases, and research on child survival and maternal health, including polio and micronutrients. The results of USAID-supported research have had significant public health impacts, starting with Oral Rehydration Salts (ORS), now used in about 85% of child diarrhea cases in almost half the world's children under 5. The results of vitamin A research now save approximately 1 million pre-school aged children a year.

And, the impact of zinc, another USAID research product, on decreasing child mortality could be as or more significant than vitamin A. By 2004, 2.5 billion autodisable syringes and 900 million vaccine vial monitors, both results of USAID-supported research, had been sold or distributed worldwide. USAID-funded research has resulted in food fortification programs, making fortified sugar, cooking oil and flours available to the majorities of the population of many countries. More recently, USAID research on natural family planning has resulted in the development of two new methods, both of which have shown to be very effective when used correctly.

USAID supported large-scale efficacy trials of insecticide treated nets (ITNs) across Africa, which provided definitive data on the highly effective impact of ITNs for preventing malaria among the most vulnerable populations of women and children. This report further details the impact of research in many other areas.

USAID invests in research to identify and assess key health problems affecting populations in developing countries and to develop and introduce new vaccines, tools, and approaches to help resolve these problems.

The objective of almost half of USAID research activities is to find ways to "introduce" and make life-saving interventions accessible to those most in need—children under 5, mothers, people living with or at risk of HIV/AIDS and TB, and women and men of reproductive age. The other objectives of USAID research activities are to identify or assess major public health problems and develop a new tool or approach to help resolve these problems.

Other partners complement the different roles that USAID plays in the cycle from research to implementation.

In some cases, for example research to develop a malaria vaccine, the objective of U.S. Government partners is different from that of USAID—a short-term vaccine to protect troops versus a long-term vaccine to protect vulnerable women and children. In the case of Oral Rehydration Salts and Vitamin A, USAID's role began with the identification of the problem and the development of the intervention, right up to wide scale introduction, working with WHO and UNICEF.

USAID's research role in yet other cases is to provide information necessary to the private sector to carry out large scale commercialization of new products such as fortified foods and long-lasting insecticide treated bed nets.

USAID's role in the development of microbicides, for example, is to focus research and development on safe, effective and acceptable microbicides to prevent HIV infection that have the appropriate cost and product characteristics for use in developing countries and, in some cases, offer dual-protection as a family planning method. USAID collaborates with NIH, CDC, and FDA to develop the U.S. Government's Strategic Plan for Microbicides.

This report details research that USAID has supported and its results. In some of the newer areas of research the report also looks at ongoing studies. One example of these is a soon-to-be commissioned review by Brian Sharp, Medical Research Council, Durban, South Africa, and Christian Lengeler, Swiss Tropical Institute, Basel, Switzerland, to compare indoor residual spraying (IRS) and ITNs across a range of malaria transmission settings in sub-Saharan Africa in terms of cost-effectiveness, impact on health measures, and operational constraints. The report, expected in early 2006, should provide clear, evidence-based guidance to

National Malaria Control Programs and USAID missions on key factors to consider when selecting vector control interventions to ensure maximum public health effectiveness for money spent. Another example is the ongoing research on simple low-cost community care packages (warming, delayed bathing) that could reduce neonatal deaths by an average of 40 percent in low resource settings.

Section I

The six research areas included in Section I account for the majority of USAID health-related research and results over the past two decades. Section I describes each area and explains how it was identified. It also describes the role of USAID, its coordination with U.S. government agencies and other partners, and the main results of the research investment to date.

The six research areas are:

1) Vaccine development
2) Maternal, newborn, and child health interventions
3) Microbicides
4) Contraceptive technologies
5) Malaria
6) Tuberculosis

1. VACCINE DEVELOPMENT

Malaria Vaccine: USAID's research role is to speed the development of malaria vaccines to protect children and pregnant women from death and serious disease in malaria-endemic areas. USAID has had a critical catalytic role in moving the current set of vaccine candidates through the research process to field trials. As a result of USAID's investments over the years, two vaccine candidates are currently undergoing safety or efficacy trials in the field. USAID works with DOD partners such as the Walter Reed Army Institute of Research and the Naval Medical Research Center; HHS partners such as the National Institutes of Health (NIH), the Centers for Disease Control and Prevention (CDC), and the Food and Drug Administration; and the Malaria Vaccine Initiative, a Bill & Melinda Gates Foundation funded program.

HIV/AIDS Vaccine: USAID's research role accelerates the development and introduction of new vaccine candidates and technologies and helps link vaccine designers with manufacturers and developing-country sites suitable for testing promising HIV vaccine candidates. USAID supports HIV vaccine research as well as policy analysis and other work to pave the way for introducing vaccines when they become available. USAID works with the

International AIDS Vaccine Initiative and the Partnership for AIDS Vaccine Evaluation (the U.S. government HIV vaccine coordination group) and would like to be involved with the Global HIV/AIDS Vaccine Enterprise as it unfolds.

Childhood Vaccines—Rotavirus and Pneumococcal Conjugate Vaccines: USAID's research role is to catalyze and coordinate clinical trials of refined rotavirus vaccine and a large-scale clinical trial of pneumococcal conjugate vaccine. USAID works with the World Health Organization (WHO), National Institutes of Health (NIH), Centers for Disease Control and Prevention (CDC), the British Medical Research Council, the London School of Hygiene and Tropical Medicine, the Program for Appropriate Technology in Health (PATH), and vaccine manufacturers. USAID's participation and investment in the Global Alliance for Vaccines and Immunization (GAVI) supported the selection of these two vaccines for a new approach to accelerated vaccine development and introduction in developing countries.

Vaccine- and Injection-Related Technologies: USAID anticipated the need for technologies that could prevent syringe and needle reuse and supported the development and introduction of the devices now known as auto-disable (AD) syringes and vaccine vial monitors (VVMs) to ensure that only potent vaccine is used. USAID works with WHO; the United Nations Children's Fund (UNICEF); PATH; Becton, Dickinson and Company; Pfizer Inc.; and GAVI. To date, 2.5 billion AD syringes and 904 million VVMs have been sold or distributed worldwide.

2. MATERNAL, NEWBORN, AND CHILD HEALTH INTERVENTIONS

Maternal and Neonatal Health: Since the launch of the Safe Motherhood Initiative in 1987, USAID has supported the development and testing of new technologies and community and facility approaches as well as meta-analyses to improve and transform maternal and neonatal interventions. USAID coordinates with WHO; host governments; U.S. and developing-country researchers; NGOs/PVOs and universities in Nepal, Bangladesh, Egypt, Tanzania, Thailand, Pakistan, India, Peru, and Malawi; the World Bank; and the American College of Nurse Midwives. Some USAID-supported technologies and approaches—the home-based maternal record, for example—now are used in countries around the world, while others are still in the development and introduction stages.

Oral Rehydration Salts, Oral Rehydration Therapy: USAID supported research to develop and introduce oral rehydration salts (ORS) and oral rehydration therapy (ORT) to treat dehydration caused by diarrhea, especially the early development research undertaken by the International Centre for Diarrheal Disease Research, Bangladesh (ICDDR,B). With support from USAID and other donors, ORS became the cornerstone of the WHO/UNICEF Program on Control of Diarrheal Diseases. In 33 countries containing almost half the world's children under age 5, use of ORS/ORT increased from about 33 percent of cases in 1990 to 85 percent by mid-decade. USAID recently supported WHO and other research partners in refining the ORS formulation. The new formulation, called reduced-osmolarity ORS, further reduces the need for intravenous therapy and is safe for treating both children and adults. UNICEF and WHO have adopted the new formulation as the global standard.

Micronutrients—Zinc: USAID-supported research built the evidence base that led to WHO and UNICEF signing a 2004 agreement revising the protocol for using zinc supplements to treat diarrhea. USAID is supporting work to introduce zinc into programs and is working with host governments to accelerate the adoption of the new recommendations for diarrhea treatment. USAID also supports product supply, guideline development, program planning, and marketing. USAID has supported the development of zinc formulations by manufacturers in a way that ensures thermostability in hot weather environments and under poor storage conditions. USAID works with WHO, the Johns Hopkins University Bloomberg School of Public Health, ICDDR,B, local universities, and international NGOs.

Micronutrients—Vitamin A: USAID supported the research that estab-lished the base of evidence for the discovery that two cents worth of vitamin A given to children every six months could reduce child mortality by 34 percent and fatality from measles by more than 50 percent, as well as reduce the severity of diarrhea and malaria. USAID continues to support research on the effects of vitamin A on maternal health and pregnancy risk. UNICEF, with procurement largely funded by the Canadian International Development Agency, now delivers 600 million to 800 million vitamin A supplements each year, saving the lives of approximately 1 million preschool children every year. More than 60 countries around the world have implemented vitamin A supplementation.

Food Fortification: USAID supported assessment research on vitamin A deficiency and anemia prevalence and the development and introduction research necessary for large-scale food fortification programs. This research has included stability and acceptability tests, technology trials, and stability trials and has resulted in food fortification programs that have made fortified sugar, cooking oils, and/or flours available to the majority of the populations of Bangladesh, Nicaragua, Philippines, Zambia, Uganda, Eritrea, Morocco, West Bank/Gaza, and Ghana. USAID works with health, industry, and food ministries; bureaus of standards; the World Food Program; national associations of food producers, millers, growers, etc.; UNICEF, the Pan American Health Organization; the Micronutrient Initiative; and local universities.

3. MICROBICIDES

USAID supports research for the development of safe, effective, and acceptable microbicides that have the appropriate cost and product characteristics for use by women in developing countries to prevent HIV infection. This research program is coordinated through collaborations with other U.S. government agencies, including NIH, CDC, and FDA, as well as other bilateral and multilateral donors, and both national and international organizations that are supporting or conducting activities related to microbicide research and development. These collaborations maximize efficiency and progress through the coordination of scientific plans, joint priority setting, sharing of resources, and learning through new data and experience. About three quarters of USAID funding supports essential phase III clinical studies that are currently underway. The remaining quarter supports developing capacity at sites for future clinical studies, research on selected second-generation microbicide candidates, and product introduction issues.

4. CONTRACEPTIVE TECHNOLOGIES

USAID supports development research to improve existing and develop new contraceptive technologies and to identify and test innovative approaches to improving the effectiveness and efficiency of family planning (and related reproductive health) service delivery. USAID also supports introduction research to expand the variety of effective contraceptive methods available in USAID-supported family planning programs worldwide. USAID works with the Eastern Virginia Medical School; Family Health International; the Population Council; Georgetown University; PATH; WHO; CDC; NIH; FDA; the United Nations Population Fund; the U.K. Department for International Development; the Bill & Melinda Gates Foundation; the Hewlett Packard, Rockefeller, and Buffet foundations; Pfizer Inc.; Wyeth; Ortho-McNeil Pharmaceutical; Schering AG; and Organon. USAID-supported research has resulted in the availability of a wider variety of new contraceptives and improvements in the understanding of existing technology.

5. MALARIA

In addition to malaria vaccine development, USAID supports research to assess the feasibility, acceptability, safety, and impact of malaria prevention and treatment technologies and to monitor the spread of drug-resistant malaria. USAID also supports research to develop new drugs for treating both uncomplicated and severe malaria and new technologies for improved home management of malaria. In the 1990s, USAID supported early clinical trials of artemisinin-based combination therapy (ACT) in children in Africa. ACT is now the WHO-recommended treatment for malaria and is being rolled out throughout Africa. USAID is now funding operations research to evaluate the introduction of new ACT treatments in sub-Saharan Africa. USAID also supported groundbreaking trials of insecticide-treated mosquito nets (ITNs) that demonstrated they can reduce under-5 mortality from all causes by about 20 percent and reduce clinical cases of malaria by 40 percent to 50 percent. ITNs are now being scaled up and used throughout Africa. Malaria research is carried out through a variety of organizations, including WHO, CDC, the Medicines for Malaria Venture, the Kenan Institute of Asia, and U.S. Pharmacopeia.

6. TUBERCULOSIS

USAID supports research in areas critical for accelerating the introduction and global expansion of the DOTS (directly observed treatment, short course) strategy and improving DOTS program performance. USAID focuses on the development, evaluation, and introduction of new diagnostics, drug regimens, and approaches that will improve the DOTS strategy and are appropriate for use in low-resource countries, including effective approaches to TB-HIV co-infection. USAID's early support of the "ProTest" approaches to TB-HIV co-infection resulted in workable models for addressing co-infection that are now being scaled up in multiple countries in Africa and are also included in the WHO and Stop TB Partnership guidance on TB-HIV. USAID also supported clinical trials on TB drug regimens of the International Union Against Tuberculosis and Lung Disease (the Union).

The study's results, published in October 2004, confirmed that a six-month course of treatment with a specific set of drugs was more effective than an alternate eight-month course with other drugs. These results are now included in the *International Standards of Care for TB Treatment*. USAID is currently supporting the development of new drugs in partnership with the Global Alliance for TB Drug Development. USAID's TB research partners include WHO; CDC; the Union; the TB Diagnostics Initiative at the Special Program for Research and Training in Tropical Diseases (a WHO/UNICEF/World Bank program); Johns Hopkins University; the University of Alabama, Birmingham; and the Global Alliance.

Section II

Fast Facts and Trends, 2002-2004

- USAID invests 6 to 7 percent of its total health-related budget in research and development. This percentage represented approximately $112 million in 2002, $123 million in 2003, and $155 million in 2004 (Table II.1).

- The proportion of funding obligated to research ranges from around 5 percent for child survival and maternal health (CS/MH),[1] to between 5 and 10 percent for HIV/AIDS and family planning and reproductive health (FP/RH), to between 10 and 15 percent for infectious diseases (ID)

  From 2002 to 2004, the total amount of funding for research grew from $112 million to $155 million. The health issue or disease with the largest single share of that funding for all three years was HIV/AIDS (37%, 37%, 46%), followed in descending order by Family Planning/Reproductive Health (29%, 32%, 24%), Child Survival, Maternal Health, including Polio and Micronutrients (14%, 15%, 14%), Malaria (7%, 7%, 7%), TB (6%, 5%, 5%), and AMR, Surveillance and Other ID (7%, 4%, 3%).

  While USAID/Washington centrally manages the largest number of research activities, the proportion of research managed by USAID missions increased from 15 percent of activities in 2002 to 21 percent in 2004

- Introduction research is the largest share of research activities (45 percent); assessment and development research are at about the same level, around 27 to 28 percent (Figure II.8).

- USAID missions originate the majority of assessment research activities (60 percent missions, 40 percent USAID/Washington) (Figure II.8).

- USAID/Washington originates the majority of development research activities (75 percent USAID/Washington, 25 percent USAID missions) and introduction research activities (65 percent USAID/Washington, 35 percent USAID missions).

- The recipients of USAID's research investments include collaborating agencies and partners such as grantees and contractors; universities; NGOs/PVOs; host governments; the Centers for Disease Control and Prevention; the National Institutes of Health; and the Department of Defense.

---

[1]This percentage is lowered by the GAVI funds included in this overall account (between $55 and $65 million)

Amount/Percent of Health or Disease Area Funding Used for Research, FY 2002-2004

Health or Disease Area	2002		2003		2004	
	$ Mil	Percent of Total Funding	$ Mil	Percent of Total Funding	$ Mil	Percent of Total Funding
HIV/AIDS	$41	8%	$46	7%	$72	6%
Family Planning/Reproductive Health	$33	7%	$40	9%	$38	9%
Infectious Diseases (inclusive of AMR/other ID, malaria, TB)	$23	12%	$20	11%	$23	11%
Child Survival/Maternal Health (inclusive of polio and micronutrients)	$16	4%	$18	5%	$22	5%
Vulnerable Children	$0	0.06%		0%	$1	7%
Total Obligation on Research	**$112**	**7%**	**$123**	**6%**	**$155**	**7%**

Distribution of Total USAID Health-Related Research Funding by Each Major Health or Disease Area

Health or Disease Area	2002	2003	2004
HIV/AIDS	37%	37%	46%
Family Planning/Reproductive Health	29%	32%	24%
Infectious Diseases (inclusive of AMR/other ID, malaria, TB)	20%	16%	15%
Child Survival/Maternal Health (inclusive of polio and micronutrients)	14%	15%	14%
Vulnerable Children	0.02%	0%	0%
Total	100%	100%	100%

Appendix G

USAID Agricultural and Natural Resources Management Research Priorities Desktop Review[1]

EXECUTIVE SUMMARY

This report gives a partial overview of current thinking by key donors, universities, and research organizations on development and research priorities in agricultural and natural resources management. It is intended to assist USAID in identifying the priority topics that would warrant Agency support in order to achieve the greatest impact on smallholder-oriented agricultural growth and rural development. There is an emerging consensus within the donor community that research on agricultural and natural resources management problems should play a key role in helping to meet the Millennium Development Goals (MDG). For example, last year's June 2004 G8 Action Plan "recognizes the essential contribution of agricultural research to the MDGs, and calls on its members to develop agricultural science and technology, in order to raise agricultural productivity, particularly in Africa." This broad agreement about means and ends does not translate easily into prescriptions for funding the "best," the most productive, or the most profitable agricultural or NRM activities, particularly with respect to research. There are a wide range of potential research directions to investigate, depending upon site-specific conditions, as well as the quality of national levels of education and connectivity, appropriateness of enabling policies, the strength of supporting financial, entrepreneurial, and physical infrastructure, the relative degree of institutional strength, and donors' funding and programmatic priorities.

---

[1]International Resources Group. Agriculture and Natural Resources Management Research Priorities Desktop Review, Washington, DC, July 2005.

Global research themes were identified and organized by development-oriented criteria, resulting in four broad categories:

- Macro policies that enable growth to take place;
- Technologies that provide new growth opportunities;
- Policies, institutions, and technologies that sustain the natural resource base;
- Policies and institutions that enable economic growth and natural resources management to be pro-poor. Efforts are needed in all of these four areas to achieve sustainable results.

These broad areas were then addressed differently within regions, and it was only within the regional context that prioritization of narrower research objectives was generally presented, as follows:

- In Asia, water use and on-farm water management, income diversification through high-value commodities, productivity of staple foods in less-favored areas, and natural resources management were most frequently addressed.
- In Latin America and the Caribbean, access to markets by the poor, land and property rights and access to rural finance, and natural resources management were key topics.
- In Central and West Asia and North Africa, water use and on-farm water management, crop improvements both for staple commodities and high value crops, income diversification, and access to infrastructure and services, as well as natural resources management were emphasized.
- In Sub-Saharan Africa, greater priority was placed on markets (including access for the poor and links to regional and international markets), water and soil technologies and practices, and crop and animal systems technologies.

The main research areas that emerged as recommended opportunities are:

- Human and institutional capacity-building
- Policies and institutions that help to create pro-growth environments
- Resource access and broadened participation
- New tools (including biotechnology) for genetic enhancement to solve the most difficult plant and animal problems of biotic and abiotic stress and of food quality
- Soil and water use and management
- Staple food crops and livestock in less-favored areas, supported by effective soil and water use and on-farm management of these resources, together with market development.
- Income diversification through High-Valued Commodities (HVC) to in-

clude fish and livestock, relevant soil/water use/on-farm management, food quality and safety, with value chains influencing respective markets.

These areas are not presented in a rank order. As a group, the listed topics have been considered for portfolio balance. They are listed individually to emphasize the importance of each topic, but several would often, if not usually be implemented as integrated research packages to enhance likelihood of adoption and broad impact, nearly always through partnership organizations. The specific topics within these broad categories would be differently arrayed in each region. The team sees research in all seven areas as essential to building a research portfolio with the ultimate goal of contributing to sustainable development that enhances agricultural productivity while also sustaining the natural resource base.

Appendix H

Examples of USAID Support for Science and Technology-Related Programs

USAID has provided the following information about its programs.

HEALTH

Demographic and Health Survey—HIV. For more than 30 years USAID has supported the collection, analysis, and use of data on international population and health through the MEASURE project's Demographic and Health Survey (DHS) and other data collection mechanisms. The first time an HIV-testing element was included in a DHS was in Mali in 2001. The Mali Ministry of Health's objective in adding testing was to estimate the rate of HIV prevalence at both the national and the regional levels. The resulting data have provided information on nationally representative HIV seroprevalence levels that is helping guide Mali in its resource allocation and decisions on HIV/AIDS policy and programs. Since the addition of the testing element was both cost-effective and efficient, other countries have added testing to their surveys. For example, following the survey in Mali, the MEASURE DHS+ project added HIV testing in Zambia and the Dominican Republic.

Micronutrients—Zinc. USAID-supported research built the evidence base that led to WHO and UNICEF signing a 2004 agreement to revise the protocol for using zinc supplements to treat diarrhea. USAID is working with host governments to accelerate the adoption of the new recommendations for diarrhea treatment. USAID also assists with product supply, guideline development, and program planning. USAID has supported the development of zinc formulations by manufacturers in a way that ensures thermo-stability in hot-weather environments and under poor storage conditions.

River Blindness—Onchocerciasis. USAID joined other donors and national governments to establish the Onchocerciasis Control Program that began in 1974. In contributing $75 million to the Onchocerciasis Trust Fund, USAID became its largest donor. In 1974, as many as 10 percent of the people in severely affected regions were blind, and 30 percent had severe visual handicaps. Farmers had begun leaving their fields amid a growing realization that something associated with the rivers was causing blindness. The program set out to eliminate the disease and to ensure that West African countries could continue disease monitoring after its elimination; these two goals have largely been achieved. Initially the control program focused on spraying of larvicide to kill black flies, but in 1988 it began to distribute the anti-parasite drug ivermectin, which Merck offered free of charge. WHO marked the end of the Onchocerciasis Control Program in West Africa in 2002. According to WHO, 600,000 cases of the disease have been prevented under the program, allowing 18 million people to grow up free of the threat of river blindness. Thousands of farmers are starting to reclaim 25 million hectares of fertile river land—enough to feed 17 million people—in areas where they once feared being struck blind.

Safe Water System. Working with the Centers for Disease Control and Prevention (CDC) and other partners, USAID has developed systems for providing low-cost technologies to improve household drinking water. More than a billion people lack access to clean water, and many more drink water contaminated by unsafe storage and handling, as well as by unsafe treatment and distribution systems. The safe water system involves a point-of-use treatment technology, safe storage in specially designed containers, and improved hygiene practices. Trials by CDC suggest that this approach can reduce the incidence of diarrhea by about 50 percent. The program was important during the aftermath of the recent tsunami when safe water solution and storage vessels were distributed in Indonesia, India, and Myanmar. The system has also been helpful in protecting vulnerable populations in hospitals and clinics.

SoloShot Syringe. USAID supported the development by PATH (Program for Appropriate Technology in Health) of SoloShot, the first auto-disposable syringe for use in developing countries. These syringes protect against the transmission of blood-borne diseases. While other disposable syringes had been in use around the world, in developing countries they were often reused without being adequately sterilized. The SoloShot is a single-use injection device designed to inactivate automatically after a single cycle of filling and injection. The syringe has a fixed needle that automatically becomes non-reusable after a single injection. Once filled, the plunger stops and cannot be pulled back. After the vaccine is injected the plunger automatically locks so that neither the needle nor the syringe can be reused. The World Health Organization called for the design of such devices in 1987. These are the only such devices that UNICEF now provides. In 2004 UNICEF distributed 400 million of them.

AGRICULTURE

Agriculture Extension in Armenia. USAID has supported a grassroots agriculture extension partnership in Armenia, connecting several U.S. assistance programs. The School Connectivity program, for example, provides computers to secondary schools across Armenia; these computers are used by students during the day and made available to the public in the evening for a small fee. Local farmers use this equipment to communicate with researchers at the Armenian Academy of Agriculture and obtain practical solutions to their agriculture problems. Plant diseases and remedies are described by means of e-mail messages, pests are photographed with digital cameras and sent directly to researchers for identification, and sources of needed supplies are compared and discussed. Farmers obtain quick answers to their questions, and researchers keep in touch with agricultural problems that need solutions.

Rust-Resistant Wheat Varieties: Leaf rust is the most widespread disease of spring bread wheat and is a major source of biological stress. Through a breeding program involving interacting genes from rust-resistant varieties, the International Maize and Wheat Improvement Center (CIMMYT), with USAID support, developed new varieties that have limited disease losses to insignificant levels in farm yields. One estimate is that the economic benefits from using these resistant varieties during the period 1973-1997 exceeded $5.3 billion based on the value of grain that farmers would have lost. From another viewpoint, there were economic, health, and environmental benefits from not having to apply fungicides on the wheat.

Prediction of Forage Conditions in East Africa. A suite of technologies have been created to predict forage conditions in arid regions of East Africa. Such early warning of impending problems are made 90 to 180 days in advance of human recognition of problems allowing for shifts in sizes of herds and other strategies to reduce livestock losses. The basis for the predictions includes simulation models that link biophysical models with satellite weather information and with data from land monitoring stations. The area of interest provides grazing for 40 million cattle, 30 million sheep, and 32 million goats.

Insect-Resistant Potato. USAID has supported research that led to a potato that resists the potato tuber moth, a pest causing significant damage to potatoes in the field and in storage. This development was achieved by engineering a novel insect resistant gene into a variety of potatoes grown by small holder farmers in developing countries. The new variety is undergoing a complete regulatory review for initial commercial release in South Africa.

ENERGY

Power Pool in South Africa. USAID was instrumental in creating the South African Power Pool, the first regional power market set up outside North America and Western Europe. Established in 1995 under the auspices of the Southern African Development Community (SADC), the power market pools the resources of 12 countries with more than 200 million people. By importing and exporting energy within the region, individual countries have been able to reduce the need to build new generation facilities. Such savings are estimated to have reached $3 billion. USAID has worked closely with other donors, including the World Bank, NORAD, and SIDA, to assist in developing and managing the power pool. Donor assistance has helped reduce the technical, legal, institutional, and political barriers to trading. Previously all power trading was done with the use of bilateral contracts that were often difficult to administer.

Transmission System Planning in Southeast Europe. USAID introduced regional electric power transmission system planning to further the development of a regional electricity market. Transmission system planning software and related training were delivered to participating countries. Transmission systems are complex, and planning is crucial when common software is used by all parties. Also adequate training is essential. USAID has been able to couple infrastructure development investments (providing the needed software) with human capacity-building. Electric power utilities in the region are now able to conduct complicated planning studies without donor assistance.

Reducing Distribution Losses in the Philippines. Visayan Electric Company (VECO) developed a USAID-sponsored partnership with Portland General Electric (PGE) designed to share best practices on a voluntary basis. They carried out a joint review of how to reduce losses on an electric power distribution system. With the U.S. partner providing the technical expertise, VECO has reduced average outages per customer from 71 hours per year to 21 hours per year. It has also reduced the duration of the average outage by 61 percent. In doing so, VECO has dramatically reduced its emergency response time, leading to improved delivery of health care, public safety, and economic development.

ENVIRONMENT

Air Monitoring in the Czech Republic. USAID provided funding to the U.S. Environmental Protection Agency to establish an air-monitoring network and conduct joint research with Czech counterparts on elevated air emissions and their adverse affects on human health in the heavily polluted region of northern Bohemia. This area, along with adjacent industrial areas of Poland and East Germany, were known as the "Black Triangle." The results showed that high exposures to air pollution could affect genetic material, reproductive functions, and early childhood vulnerability to infections. The Czech government thereupon decided to accelerate its program to convert home heating from coal to gas by establishing a special allocation of 6 billion Czech crowns ($240 million at the time) to cover consumer costs of fuel conversion.

Drought-Famine Early Warning in the Sahel. The Famine Early Warning Systems Network (FEWS NET) issues alerts for 25 African countries indicating anomalies in weather or other potential climate shocks that could result in loss of production and subsequent food insecurity. Since the late 1980s, the early availability of reliable information has enabled planners in the governments, USAID, U.N. agencies, and NGOs to put into motion early decision-making to prepare food and survey teams to respond to impending famine threats. The countries themselves can field the first sets of emergency responders while modifying policies to improve access to food for their citizens.

Appendix I

Recent National Academies Reports Relevant to Science and Technology in Development

Improving Birth Outcomes: Meeting the Challenge in the Developing World, Board on Global Health, 2003.

Scaling Up Treatment for the Global AIDS Pandemic: Challenges and Opportunities, Board on Global Health, 2004.

Saving Lives, Buying Time: Economics of Malaria Drugs in an Age of Resistance, Board on Global Health, 2004.

Healers Abroad: Americans Responding to the Human Resource Crises in HIV/ AIDS, Board on Global Health, 2005.

Political Implications of International Graduate Students and Postdoctoral Scholars in the United States, Policy and Global Affairs Division, 2005.

Science and Technology in Armenia: Toward a Knowledge-Based Economy, Policy and Global Affairs Division, 2004.

Growing Up Global: The Changing Transitions to Adulthood in Developing Countries. Division of Behavioral and Social Sciences and Education, 2005.

Appendix J

Recent National Academies Activities Relevant to Science and Technology in Development

Review of *The President's Emergency Plan for AIDS Relief (PEPFAR): Implementation and Evaluation*, Board on Global Health (funded by the Department of State).

Implementation of a program of *S&T Capacity Building in Africa*, Policy and Global Affairs Division (funded by the Bill & Melinda Gates Foundation).

Support for *USAID Research Programs: US-Israel Cooperative Development Research Program and the Middle East Regional Cooperation Program*, Policy and Global Affairs Division (funded by USAID).

Implementation of *U.S.-Pakistan Science and Technology Cooperative Program*, Policy and Global Affairs Division (funded by USAID).

Roundtable on Natural Disasters, Division on Environment and Life Sciences (funded by a number of public and private organizations).

Implementation of *The Grainger Prize for a New Technology for Removing Arsenic from Drinking Water in Developing Countries*, National Academy of Engineering (funded by the Grainger Foundation).

Implementation of a program of *Graduate Training in the United States for Young Vietnamese Scientists and Engineers*, Policy and Global Affairs Division (funded by the Vietnam Foundation).

Appendix K

Pakistan-U.S. Science and Technology Cooperative Program 2005

PROJECTS SELECTED FOR JOINT FUNDING

Development of a Strategic Model for Improvement of Construction Project Management Education, Research, and Practice in Pakistan
Syed Mahmood Ahmed, Florida International University
Sarosh Hashmat Lodi, NED University of Engineering and Technology

Development of Guidelines for Asphalt Pavement Recycling in Pakistan
Gilbert Y. Baladi, Michigan State University
Tayyeb Akram, National University of Sciences and Technology

Development of Computational Mechanics Infrastructure and Human Resources for Advancing Engineering Design Practices in Pakistani Industry
Arif Masud, University of Illinois at Chicago
Abdullah Sadiq, Ghulam Ishaq Khan Institute of Engineering Science and Technology

Establishment of Extrusion Center of the Institute of Food Science and Technology, University of Agriculture, Faisalabad
Mian Nadeem Riaz, Texas Engineering Experiment Station
Faqir Muhammad Anjum, University of Agriculture

Gene Pyramiding through Genetic Engineering for Increased Salt Tolerance in Wheat
Eduardo Blumwald, University of California, Davis
Anjuman Arif, National Institute for Biotechnology and Genetic Engineering

Understanding and Control of Plant Viral Disease Complexes in Pakistan
Claude M. Fauquet, Donald Danforth Plant Science Center
Shahid Mansoor, National Institute for Biotechnology and Genetic Engineering

Determination of Heavy Metals and Polycyclic Aromatic Hydrocarbons in Airborne Particulates in Lahore, Pakistan, and Madison, Wisconsin, USA
James Jay Schauer, University of Wisconsin-Madison
Tauseef A. Quraishi, University of Engineering and Technology

Antimicrobial Resistance in Pakistan: A Program to Develop and Strengthen Capacity for Surveillance, Containment, and Diagnosis through Public-Private Sector Partnership
Mary Brandt, Centers for Disease Control and Prevention
Rumina Hasan, The Aga Khan Medical University

Intensification of Forensic Services and Research at Centre for Applied Molecular Biology
Mohammad Ashraf Tahir, Strand Analytical Laboratories, LLC
Sheikh Riazuddin, Centre for Applied Molecular Biology

Improving the Lifestyle of Villagers in Remote Areas of the Federally Administered Tribal Areas of Pakistan Using Renewable Energy
Johnny Weiss, Solar Energy International
Ishtiaq A. Qazi, National University of Sciences and Technology

Capacity Building for Research, Education, and Training in Water Resources Management in Pakistan
M. Hanif Chaudhry, University of South Carolina
Muhammad Latif, University of Engineering and Technology

Appendix L

Description of USAID
Recruitment Programs

AGENCY EXPLAINS HOW TO GET A JOB AT USAID[1]

It's late fall, and many graduates are wondering how to apply for work at USAID. Here is a brief introduction to the kind of background, education, and job experience the Agency is looking for as it seeks to fill positions that become open each year.

USAID recruitment is a year-round process. At the Office of Human Resources, efforts focus mainly on attracting new foreign service officers at junior and mid-levels.

On the foreign service (FS) side, recruiters are looking for candidates with a wide range of master's degrees, from international relations to public health. People with law degrees and doctoral candidates can also apply.

> The only way to apply for a job at USAID is on the internet. Jobs are advertised on USAID's website at regular intervals during the year, and prospective applicants are encouraged to log on frequently.

Experience is also considered. For FS candidates, overseas experience is almost always a must. Working for the Peace Corps, a nongovernmental organization, international organization, or for-profit contractor overseas can provide valuable experience.

---

[1]USAID Front Lines, Nov. 2005.(see www.usaid.gov/press/frontlines)

FS candidates can apply for one or two tracks. For both programs, USAID advises candidates to expect to be based overseas for most of their careers.

- **New Entry Professional (NEP) Program.** Typically, successful candidates for this mid-level track have five to seven years' development experience overseas plus a master's degree. NEPs normally spend 12–18 months in Washington, D.C., before being assigned overseas.
- **International Development Intern (IDI) Program.** While previous work experience is not required, most successful applicants have one to two years' overseas experience. Students need to apply while in graduate school or within a year after completing graduate school. IDIs can expect to be assigned overseas roughly six months after joining USAID.

Potential applicants should know that the FS hiring process—from submitting an application to coming on duty—can take up to a year. Security clearance, medical clearance, and other factors can contribute to this length of time.

USAID also hires many civil service employees to work in Washington, D.C. These openings are advertised on an individual basis.

The Presidential Management Fellows (PMF) Program is another entry to the civil service for people with recent master's degrees. USAID is the second largest employer of PMFs in the federal government.

There are also Foreign Service Limited Appointments. These are five-year appointments and, generally, not career tracks. USAID uses these to cover hard-to-fill positions.

The only way to apply for a job at USAID is on the internet. Jobs are advertised on USAID's website at regular intervals during the year, and prospective applicants are encouraged to log on frequently.